AF544709

TALES OF PRISON LIFE

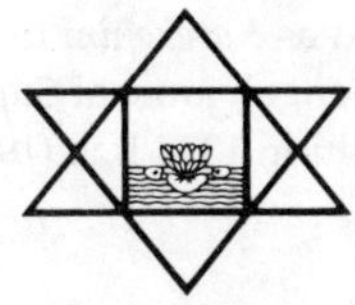

SRI AUROBINDO

Tales of Prison Life

SRI AUROBINDO ASHRAM
PONDICHERRY

Originally published as *Karakahini* in 1316 B.S. (1909-10)
in the Bengali journal *Suprabhat*
First edition 1328 B.S. (1921-22)

English translation:
First edition 1974
Fourth edition 1997
Second impression 2002

Rs. 35.00

ISBN 81-7058-495-7

Published by Sri Aurobindo Ashram Publication Department,
Pondicherry - 605 002
Printed at Sri Aurobindo Ashram Press, Pondicherry
PRINTED IN INDIA

Publisher's Note

Tales of Prison Life is Sri Aurobindo's account of his experiences as an undertrial prisoner in Alipore Jail, Calcutta. Arrested for conspiracy in May 1908, Sri Aurobindo spent one full year in jail while the British Government, in a protracted trial, tried to implicate him in various revolutionary activities. Acquitted and released May, 1909, he wrote a series of articles in Bengali in the journal *Suprabhat* describing his life in prison and the courtroom. These articles form the main text of this book.

Several briefer pieces are also included in the book: three essays in which Sri Aurobindo discusses the noble character of the young revolutionaries imprisoned with him; a poem, "Invitation", which he wrote in Alipore Jail; and a speech at Uttarapara in which he disclosed for the first time some of the spiritual experiences he had while in jail.

"The Uttarpara Speech" was spoken in English. The poem "Invitation" was written in English. The three essays and the main text were written in Bengali and appear here in translation. Further information is given in the Note on the Texts at the end of the book.

CONTENTS

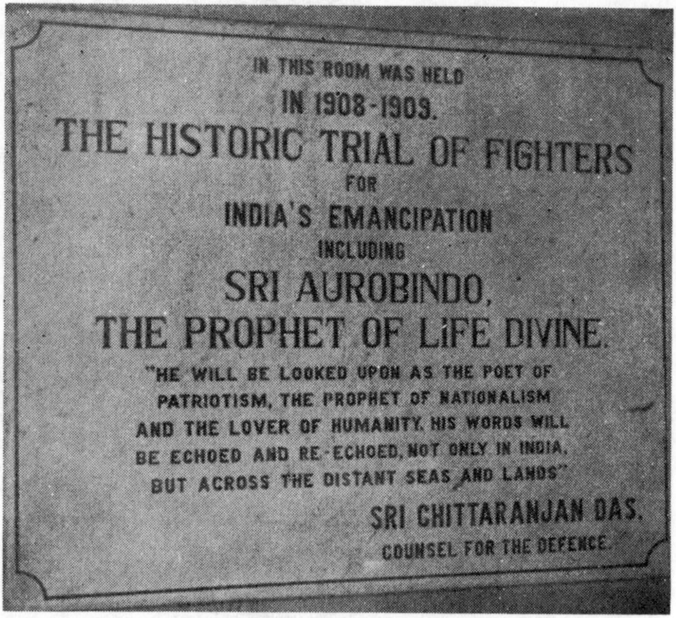

IN THIS ROOM WAS HELD
IN 1908-1909.
THE HISTORIC TRIAL OF FIGHTERS
FOR
INDIA'S EMANCIPATION
INCLUDING
SRI AUROBINDO,
THE PROPHET OF LIFE DIVINE.
"HE WILL BE LOOKED UPON AS THE POET OF
PATRIOTISM, THE PROPHET OF NATIONALISM
AND THE LOVER OF HUMANITY. HIS WORDS WILL
BE ECHOED AND RE-ECHOED, NOT ONLY IN INDIA,
BUT ACROSS THE DISTANT SEAS AND LANDS"
SRI CHITTARANJAN DAS.
COUNSEL FOR THE DEFENCE.

Alipore Court: Commemorative Plate

the four pillars of upanishads:

1 Nitya Nityanam (one eternal in many transients)

2 Chetanas chetananam (one Conciousness in many Conciousnesses)

3 So-ham (he am I)

4 A-ham brahm asim (I am brahma eternal)

vedas = anciamt scriptures.

vedas
- rig (world science) ← upanishads
- yejor (rituals) ← upanishads
- sama (music) ← upanishads
- atharva (black magic) ← upanishads

each veda is devided to 4 parts:

1 mantra-samhitas

2 brahmanas

3 aranyakas

4 upanishads

vedanta = end of vedas = based on the philosophy of or teachings of upanishads

---

*upanishads are the highest knowledge given to human-kind.

When I was asleep in the Ignorance, I came to a place of meditation full of holy men and I found their company wearisome and the place a prison; when I awoke, God took me to a prison and turned it into a place of meditation and His trysting-ground.

Thoughts and Aphorisms — Sri Aurobindo

Sri Aurobindo (1908-09)

Tales of Prison Life

On Friday, May 1, 1908, I was sitting in the *Bande Mataram* office, when Srijut Shyamsunder Chakravarty handed over a telegram from Muzaffarpur. On reading it I learned of a bomb outrage in which two European ladies had been killed. In that day's issue of the "Empire" I read another news item that the Police Commissioner had said that he knew the people involved in the murder and that they would soon be put under arrest. At that time I had no idea that I happened to be the main target of suspicion and that according to the police I was the chief killer, the instigator and secret leader of the young terrorists and revolutionaries. I did not know that that day would mean the end of a chapter of my life, and that there stretched before me a year's imprisonment during which period all my human relations would cease, that for a whole year I would have to live, beyond the pale of society, like an animal in a cage. And when I would re-enter the world of activity it would not be the old familiar Aurobindo Ghose. Rather it would be a new being, a new character, intellect, life, mind, embarking upon a new course of action that would come out of the ashram at Alipore. I have spoken of a year's imprisonment. It would have been more appropriate to speak of a year's living in a forest, in an ashram or hermitage. For long I had made a great effort for a direct vision (sakshāt darshan) of the Lord of my Heart; had entertained the immense hope of knowing the Preserver of the World, the Supreme Person (*Purushottam*) as friend and master. But due to the pull of a thousand worldly desires, the attachment towards numerous activities and the deep darkness of ignorance I did not succeed in that effort. At long last the most merciful all-good Lord (*Shiv Hari*) destroyed all these enemies at one stroke and helped me in my path, pointed to the *yogashram*, Himself staying as guru and companion in my little abode of retirement and spiritual discipline. The British prison was that ashram. I have also watched this strange contradiction in my life that however much good my well-intentioned friends might do for me, it is those who have harmed me – whom shall I call an enemy, since enemy I have none? – my opponents have helped me even more. They wanted to do me an ill turn, the result was I got what I wanted. The only result of the wrath of the British Government was that I found God. It is not the aim of these essays to provide an intimate journal of my life in the prison. I wish to mention only a few external details, but I have thought it better to mention, at least once, in the beginning, the main theme of the prison life. Else readers may think that suffering is the only item of prison life. I can't say there were no inconveniences, but on the whole the time passed quite happily.

On Friday night I was sleeping without a worry. At about five in the morning my sister rushed to my room in an agitated manner and called me out by name. I got up. The next moment the small room was filled with armed policemen; Superintendent Cregan, Mr. Clark of 24-Parganas, the charming and delightful visage of familiar Sriman Benod Kumar Gupta, a few Inspectors, red turbans, spies and search witnesses. They all came running like heroes, pistols in hand, as though they were besieging, with guns and cannon, a well-armed fort. I heard that a white hero had aimed a pistol at my sister's breast, but I did not see it. I was sitting on my bed, still half-asleep, when Cregan inquired, "Who is Aurobindo Ghose, is that you?" I answered, "Yes. I am Aurobindo Ghose." Immediately he ordered a policeman to put me under arrest. Then, because of an extremely objectionable expression used by Cregan, there was a little exchange of words between the two of us. I asked for the search warrant, read and signed it. Finding a mention of bombs in the warrant I understood that the presence of these soldiers and policemen was connected with the Muzaffarpur killing. The one thing I did not understand was why, even before any bombs or explosives had been discovered in my house, I was arrested in the absence of a body warrant. But I did not raise any useless objections. Afterwards, under instructions from Cregan, my arms were handcuffed, and a rope tied round my middle. An upcountry constable stood behind me holding the rope end. Just then the police brought in Srijut Abinash Bhattacharya and Srijut Sailen Bose, hand-cuffed and roped round the midriff. Nearly half an hour after, I do not know at whose bidding, they removed the rope and the handcuff. From Cregan's words it seemed as if he had entered into the lair of some ferocious animal, as if we were a lot of uneducated, wild lawbreakers, and it was unnecessary to speak or behave courteously towards us. But after the sharp exchange the sahib grew a little milder. Benodbabu tried to explain something about me to him. After which Cregan asked me: "It seems you are a B.A. Is it not a matter of shame for an educated person like you to be sleeping on the floor of an unfurnished room and in a house like this?" "I am a poor man, and I live like one," I said. "Then have you worked up all this mischief with the idea of becoming a rich man?" Cregan replied in a loud voice. Knowing how impossible it was to explain the love of motherland, sacrifice or the sublimity of a vow of poverty to this thick-skulled Briton I did not make the attempt.

All the while the search continued. Beginning at five-thirty, it was over at about eleven-thirty. Inside and outside the boxes, all the exercise books, letters, papers, scraps, poems, plays, prose, essays, translations, nothing escaped the clutches of the all-engrossing search. Among the witnesses to the search Mr. Rakshit seemed a little put out; later, bemoaning his lot, he informed me that the police had dragged him along, and that he had no idea that he would have to be a party to such a nefarious activity. He described, most pathetically, how he had been kidnapped for the purpose. The attitude of the other witness, Samarnath, was of quite another kind; he discharged his part of the job with considerable gusto, like a true loyalist and to the manner born. Nothing remarkable transpired in the course of the search. But I recollect Mr. Clark looking long and suspiciously at the sacred earth from Dakshineshwar that had been kept in a small cardboard box; he suspected it might be some new and terribly powerful explosive. In a sense Mr. Clark's suspicions were not unfounded. In the end the decision was reached that it was a piece of earth which it was unnecessary to send to the chemical analyst. I did not join in the search except to open a few boxes. No papers or letters were shown or read out to me. Mr. Cregan, for his own delectation, read out loudly a letter from Alakdhari. The friendly Benod Gupta in his natural and delightful style marched round the room, raising echoes everywhere and brought out from the shelf or some other corner papers or letters, and now and then muttering "Very important, very important" handed these over to Cregan. I was never told what these important documents might be. Nor was I at all curious, since I knew it was impossible that there might be in my house any formula for the manufacture of explosives or documents relating to conspiracy.

After rummaging through my room the police led us to the adjoining room. Cregan opened a box belonging to my youngest aunt; he once or twice glanced at the letters, then saying that it was no use carrying these women's correspondence, left them behind. Then the police *mahatma*s appeared on the ground floor. Cregan had his tea there. I had a cup of cocoa and toast. During this period Cregan tried to argue and convince me about his political views – this mental torture I had to suffer coolly. But may I ask, one knows physical torture to be part of the traditional police strategy, but does such inhuman mental torture also fall within the purview of its unwritten laws? I hope our highly respectable friend-of-the-country Srijut Jogeshchandra Ghose will raise this question in the Legislative Assembly.

After searching the rooms on the ground floor and the office of "Navashakti" the police again came up to the first floor to open an iron safe belonging to "Navashakti". Unable to open it after a half-hour battle, they decided to remove it bodily to the police station. This time a police officer discovered a bicycle, with a railway label bearing the mark of Kushtia. Immediately they took it as an important proof that the vehicle belonged to the man who had earlier shot a sahib there and they gladly took it away with them.

At about eleven-thirty we left our house. Outside the gates, in a car, I found my maternal uncle and Srijut Bhupendranath Basu. "On what charges have you been arrested?" asked uncle. "I know nothing," I answered. "They arrested and handcuffed me soon after getting into my room; they didn't show any body warrant." When uncle inquired why the handcuffs were thought necessary, Benodbabu said, "Sir, it's not my fault. Ask Aurobindobabu, I told the sahib and had the handcuffs removed." On Bhupenbabu's asking about my offence, Mr. Gupta mentioned the I. P. C. article on murder. Bhupenbabu was stunned and did not say another word. Later on I came to know that my solicitor, Sri Hirendranath Datta, had expressed a desire to be present on my behalf during the search. The police had turned down the request.

Benodbabu was entrusted with taking us to the police station. There he behaved with us in a remarkably decent manner. We had our bath and lunch there and then proceeded towards Lal Bazar. After being made to wait there for a couple of hours we were removed to Royd Street, in which auspicious locality we stayed all evening. It was there that I first came to know the sly detective Maulvi Shams-ul-Alam and had the pleasure of entering with him into a cordial relation. Till then the great Maulvi had not acquired either enough influence or energy, he was not yet the chief researcher in the bomb outrage or functioning as Mr. Norton's proper and unfailing *aide mémoire*. Till that time Ramsadaybabu was acting as the chief protagonist. The Maulvi made me listen to a most entertaining sermon on religion. That Hinduism and Islam have the same basic principles: in the Omkara of the Hindus we have the three syllables, A, U, M; the first three letters of the Holy Koran are A, L, M. According to philological laws, U is used for L; *ergo*, Hindus and Musulmans have the same mantra or sacred syllables. Yet one has to maintain the uniqueness of one's faith, so a Hindu considers it wrong to eat with Musulmans. To be truthful is part of the religious life. The Sahibs say Aurobindo Ghose is the leader of the terrorist party, this is a matter of shame and sorrow for India. But by keeping to the path of rectitude the situation can yet be saved. The Maulvi was fully convinced that distinguished persons, men of high character, like Bipin Pal and Aurobindo Ghose, whatever they might have done, they would openly confess these. Srijut Purnachandra Shastri, who happened to be present there, expressed his doubt in this respect. But the Maulvi did not give up his views. I was charmed and delighted with his knowledge, intelligence and religious fervour. Thinking that it would be impertinent to speak much I listened politely to his priceless sermon and cherished it in my heart. But in spite of so much religious enthusiasm the Maulvi did not give up his profession of a 'tec'. Once he said: "You made a great mistake in handing over the garden to your youngest brother to manufacture bombs. It was not very intelligent on your part." Understanding the implication of his words I smiled a little, and said: "Sir, the garden is as much mine as my brother's. Where did you learn that I had given it over to him, or given it to him for the purpose of manufacturing bombs?" A little abashed, the

Maulvi answered: "No, no, I was saying in case you have done it." Then the great-souled Maulvi opened an autobiographical chapter before me, and said, "All the moral or economic progress that I have made in life can be traced back to a single sufficing moral adage of my father. He would always say, 'Never give up an immediate gain.' This great word is the sacred formula of my life, all this advancement is owing to the fact that I have always remembered that sage advice." At the time of this pronunciamento the Maulvi stared at me so closely that it seemed as though I was his meat and food, which, following the parental advice, he would be loath to give up. In the evening, the redoubtable Ramsaday Mukhopadhyay appeared on the scene. He expressed words of unusual kindness and sympathy, told everyone present to be careful about my food and bed. Immediately afterwards some fellows came and took Sailendra and me, through rain and storm, to the lock-up at Lal Bazar. This was the only occasion when I met Ramasaday. I could see the man was both intelligent and active, but his words and demeanour, his tone, his gait, all seemed fake and unnatural, as if he was for ever acting on a stage. There are men like that whose words, bodies, actions are an embodiment of untruth. They are experts in imposing themselves on immature minds, but those who know men and their ways find them out at once.

At Lal Bazar on the ground floor in a spacious room we two were kept together. Some snacks were served. After a while two Englishmen entered the room, later I was told that one of them was the Police Commissioner Mr. Halliday himself. Finding us both together Halliday was wrathful with the sergeant, and pointing towards me he said, "Take care that nobody stays or speaks with this man." Sailen was at once removed and locked up in another room. When the others had left, Halliday asked me: "Aren't you ashamed of being involved in this cowardly, dastardly activity?" "What right have you to assume that I was involved?" To this Halliday replied: "I am not assuming, I know everything." At this I said: "What you know or do not know is your concern. I wholly deny having any connection with these murderous acts."

That night I had other visitors, all members of the police force. There was a mystery behind the visit, which till now I have failed to fathom. A month and a half before my arrest an unknown gentleman had come to see me. He said: "Sir, we have not met, but since I have great respect for you I am here to warn you of an impending danger. I would also like to know if you are familiar with anyone at Konnagar. Did you ever visit the place, and do you have a house there?" "No, I do not have any house there," I said. "But I have been there once and am known to some people there." "I will say nothing more," said the stranger, "but from now on you should not meet anyone from there. Some wicked people are conspiring against you and your brother, Barindra. Soon they will put you into trouble. Don't ask me anything more." I told him: "Sir, I am unable to understand how this incomplete information will help me, but since you come with friendly intentions, thank you very much. I do not wish to know anything more. I have complete faith in God. He will always protect me, and it is for me needless to make any attempt to be careful." I heard nothing about this afterward. That this stranger and well-wisher did not imagine things, I had proof the same night. An inspector and a few police officers came to pump out my connection with Konnagar. "Is your original home at Konnagar?" they asked. "Did you ever visit the place? When? And why? Has Barindra any properties there?" – and other questions. I answered these mainly in order to get at the root of the mystery. The attempt was not a success, but from the questions as well as the manner of the police inquiry it appeared that they had come by some information which they were trying to verify. I guessed that just as in the Tai-Maharaj Case there had been an attempt to prove Tilak a hypocrite, liar, cheat and tyrant, in which the Bombay Government had joined hands and wasted public money – similarly there were people interested in putting me into trouble.

The whole of Sunday was passed in the lock-up. There was a staircase in front of my room. In the morning I found a few young lads coming down the stairs. Their faces were unfamiliar, but I guessed that they too had been arrested in the same case. Later I came to know that these were the lads from the Manicktola Gardens. A month later, in the jail I came to know them. A little later I too was taken downstairs for a wash – since there was no arrangement for a bath, I went without it. For lunch I swallowed, with some effort, a few morsels of pulse and boiled rice. The effort proved too much and had to be given up. In the afternoon we had puffed rice. For three days this was our diet. But I must also add that on Monday the sergeant, of himself, gave me tea and toast.

Later I came to learn that my lawyer had sought permission from the Commissioner to have my food sent from home, but to this Mr. Halliday did not agree. I also heard that the accused were forbidden to consult their lawyer or attorney. I don't know if this restriction is valid or not. It is true that though a lawyer's advice would have been of help to me, I didn't quite need it; it has, however, harmed some others involved in the case. On Monday we were presented before the Commissioner. Abinash and Sailen were with me. We were taken in different batches. Thanks to our good deeds in a past incarnation we three had been arrested earlier, and, since we had already some experience of legal quibblings, all of us refused to make any declarations before the Commissioner. Next day we were taken to the court of the magistrate, Mr. Thornhill. It was then that I met for the first time Srijut Kumar Krishna Datta, Mr. Manuel, and one of my relations. Mr. Manuel asked me, "According to the police a good deal of suspicious literature has been recovered from your house. Were these papers or letters really there?" "I can say without a shadow of doubt," I told him, "that there were no such things, it is quite impossible." Of course then I did not know of the "sweets letter" or of the "scribblings". I told my relative: "Tell the people at home not to fear or worry, my innocence will be fully vindicated." From that period on I had a firm belief that it would be so. In the beginning, during solitary imprisonment, the mind was a little uneasy. But after three days of prayer and meditation an unshakable peace and faith again overwhelmed the being.

From Mr. Thornhill's court we were taken in a carriage to Alipore. The group included Nirapada, Dindayal, Hemchandra Das, and others. Of these I knew Hemchandra Das; once I had put up at his place in Midnapore. Who could have known then that I would meet him like this, as a prisoner on the way to the jail? We were detained for a little while at the Alipore magistrate's court, but we were not presented before the magistrate; they went in only to get an order signed. We again got into the carriage, when a gentleman came near me and said, "I have heard that they are planning solitary confinement for you and orders are being passed to that effect. Probably they will not allow anyone to see or meet you. If you wish to convey any information to your people, I shall do that." I thanked him, but since what I wished to convey I had already done through my relative, I did not tell him anything more. I am mentioning this fact as an example of my countrymen's sympathy and unsought kindness towards me. Thereafter from the court we went to the jail and were surrendered to its officers. Before entering the jail precincts we were given a bath, put into prison uniform, while our clothes, shirts, dhotis and *kurta*s were taken away for laundry. The bath, after four days, was a heavenly bliss. After that they took us to our respective cells. I went into mine and the doors were closed as soon as I got in. My prison life at Alipore began on May 5. The next year, on May 6, I was released.

My solitary cell was nine feet long and five feet in width; it had no windows, in front stood strong iron bars; this cage was my appointed abode. Outside was a small courtyard, with stony grounds, a high brick wall with a small wooden door. On top of that door, at eye level, there was a small hole or opening. After the door had been bolted the sentry peeped, from time to time, in order

"... this cage was my appointed abode."

to find out what the convict was doing. But my courtyard door remained open for most of the time. There were six contiguous rooms like that, in prison parlance these were known as the 'six decrees'. 'Decrees' stood for rooms for special punishment – those who are condemned to solitary imprisonment by the orders of either the judge or the jail superintendent have to stay in these mini-caves. Even in such solitary confinement there is the rule of caste or hierarchy. Those who are heavily punished have their courtyard doors permanently closed; deprived of contacts with the rest of the human world, their only point of contact with the outside world is restricted to the vigilant eyes of the sentry and the fellow-convict who brings their food twice a day. Since Hemchandra Das was looked upon as being a greater terror for the criminal investigation department than I, he had been given this strict regimen. But in the solitary cell too there are refinements – handcuffs and iron rings round one's hand and foot. This highest punishment is meted out not only for disturbing the peace of the prison or playing rough, but also if one is found frequently slack in prison labour. To harass those convicted in cases of solitary confinement is against the spirit of law, but the Swadeshi or 'Bande Mataram' convicts were beyond the pale and according as the police desired benign arrangements were made for these.

Such was the place where we were lodged. As for fittings our generous authorities had left nothing to be desired so far as our hospitable reception was concerned. One plate and bowl used to adorn the courtyard. Properly washed and cleaned, my self-sufficing plate and bowl shone like silver, it was the solace of my life. In its impeccable, glowing radiance in the 'heavenly kingdom', in that symbol of immaculate British imperialism, I used to enjoy the pure bliss of loyalty to the Crown. Unfortunately, the plate too shared in the bliss, and if one pressed one's fingers a little hard on its surface it would start flying in a circle, like the whirling dervishes of Arabia. And then one had to use one hand for eating while the other held the plate in position. Else, while whirling, it would attempt to slip away with the incomparable grub provided by the prison authorities. But more dear and useful than the plate was the bowl. Among inert objects it was like the British civilian. Just as the civilian *ipso facto* is fit and able to undertake any administrative duty, be it as judge, magistrate, police, revenue officer, chairman of municipality, professor, preacher, whatever you ask him to do he can become at your merest bidding – just as for him to be an investigator, complainant, police magistrate, even at times to be the counsel for defence, all these roles hold a friendly concourse in the same hospitable body, my dear bowl was equally multi-purpose. The bowl was free from all caste restrictions, beyond discrimination: in the prison cell it helped in the act of ablution; later with the same bowl I gargled, bathed; a little later when I had to take my food, the lentil soup or vegetable soup was poured into the same container; I drank water out of it and washed my mouth. Such an all-purpose priceless object can be had only in a British prison. Serving all my worldly needs the bowl became an aid in my spiritual discipline too. Where else could I find such an aid and preceptor to get rid of the sense of disgust? After the first spell of solitary imprisonment was over, when we were allowed to stay together, civilian's rights were bifurcated, and the authorities arranged for another receptacle for the privy. But for one month I acquired an unsought lesson in controlling my sense of disgust. The entire procedure for defecation seems to have been oriented towards the art of self-control. Solitary imprisonment, it has been said, must be counted as a special form of punishment and its guiding principle the avoidance of human company and the open sky. To arrange this ablution in the open or outside would mean a violation of that principle; hence two baskets, with tar coating, would be kept in the room itself. The sweeper (*methar*) would clean it up in the mornings and afternoons. In case of intense agitation and heart-warming speeches from our side cleaning would be done at other times too. But if one went to the privy at odd hours, as penance one had to put up with the noxious and fetid smell. In the second chapter of our solitary confinement there were some reforms in this respect, but British reforms keep the old principles intact while making minor changes in administration. Needless to say, because of all this arrangement in a small room, one had throughout to undergo considerable inconvenience, especially at meal times and during the night. Attached bathrooms are, I know, oftentimes a part of western culture, but to have, in a small cell, a bedroom, dining room and w.c. rolled into one – this is what is called too much of a good thing! We Indians are full of regrettable customs, it is painful for us to be so highly civilised.

Among household utilities there were also a small bucket, a tin water-container and two prison blankets. The small bucket would be kept in the courtyard, where I used to have my bath. In the beginning I did not suffer from water scarcity, though that happened later on. At first the convict in the neighbouring cowshed would supply water as and when I wanted it, hence during the bathing recess amidst the austerities of prison life I enjoyed every day a few moments of the householder's luxury and love of pleasure. The other convicts were not so fortunate, the same tub or pail did for the w.c., cleaning of utensils and bath. As undertrial prisoners this extraordinary luxury was allowed to them, the convicts had to take their bath in a bowlful or two of water. According to the British the love of God and physical well-being are almost equal and rare virtues, whether the prison regulations were made in order to prove the point of such a proverb or to prevent the unwilling austerity of the convicts spoilt by excessive bathing facilities, it was not easy to decide. This liberality of the authorities was made light of by the convicts "crow bathing". Men are by nature discontented. The arrangements for drinking water were even better than the bathing facilities. It was then hot summer, in my little room the wind was almost forbidden to enter. But the fierce and blazing sunlight of May had free access to it. The entire room would burn like an oven. While being locked thus the only way to lessen one's irresistible thirst was the tepid water in the small tin container. I would drink that water often, but this would not quench the thirst, rather there would be heavy sweating and soon after the thirst would be renewed. But one or two had earthen pots placed in their courtyard, for which, remembering the austerities of a past incarnation, they would count themselves lucky. This compelled even the strongest believers in personal effort to admit the role of fate; some had cold water, others remained thirsty for ever, it was as the stars decreed. But in their distribution of tin-cans or water-pots, the authorities acted with complete impartiality. Whether I was pleased or not with such erratic arrangements, the generous jail doctor found my water trouble unbearable. He made efforts to get an earthen pot for my use, but since the distribution was not in his hands he did not succeed for long; at last at his bidding the head-sweeper managed to discover an earthen pot from somewhere. Before that in course of my long battle with thirst I had achieved a thirst-free state. In this blazing room two prison blankets served for my bed. There was no pillow, so I would spread one of these as mattress and fold the other as a pillow, and sleep like that. When the heat became unbearable I would roll on the ground and enjoy it. Then did I know the joy of the cool touch of Mother Earth. But the floor's contact in the prison cell was not always pleasing, it prevented the coming of sleep and so I had to take recourse to the blanket. The days on which it rained were particularly delightful. But there was this difficulty that during rain and thunder, thanks to the violent dance *(tandava nritya)* of the strong wind, full of dust, leaf and grass, a small-scale flood would take place inside my little room. After that there was no alternative but to rush to a corner with a wet blanket. Even after this game of nature was over, till the earth dried one had to seek refuge in reflection leaving aside all hope of sleep. The only dry areas were near the w.c., but one did not feel like placing the blankets near that area. But in spite of such difficulties on windy days a lot of air also blew in and since that took away the furnace-like heat of the room I welcomed the storm and the shower.

The description of the Alipore government hotel which I have given here, and will give still more later, is not for the purpose of advertising my own hardship; it is only to show what peculiar arrangements are made for undertrial prisoners in the civilised British Raj, and what prolonged agony for the innocent. The causes of hardship that I have described were no doubt there, but since my faith in divine mercy was strong I had to suffer only for the first few days; thereafter – by what means I shall mention later – the mind had risen above these sufferings and grown incapable of feeling any hardship. That is why when I recollect my prison life, instead of anger or sorrow I feel like laughing. When first of all I had to go into my cage dressed in the odd prison uniform, and noticed the arrangements for our stay, this was what I felt. And I laughed within myself. Having studied the history of the English people and their recent doings I had already found out their strange and mysterious character. So I was not at all astonished or unhappy at their behaviour towards me. Normally this kind of behaviour towards us would be considered extremely illiberal and blameworthy. We all came from gentlemanly stock; many were scions of landlords; some were, in terms of their family, education, quality and character, the equals of the highest classes in England. The charge on which we had been arrested, that too was not ordinary murder, theft or dacoity; it was an attempt at insurrection to liberate the country from foreign yoke or conspiracy tending towards armed conflict. The main cause of our detention was suspicion on the part of the police, though even there in many instances the proof of guilt was wholly wanting. In such cases to be herded together like ordinary thieves and dacoits – and not even as thieves and dacoits, to keep them like animals in a cage, to give them food unfit for animals, to make them endure water scarcity, thirst and hunger, sun, rain and cold, all these do not enhance the glory of the British race and its imperial officers. This is, however, a national defect of their character. The English are possessed of the qualities of the Kshatriya, but in dealing with enemies or opponents they are cent per cent businesslike. But, at the time, I was not annoyed at this. On the contrary, I had felt a little happy that no discrimination had been made between the common uneducated masses and myself; moreover, the arrangement added fuel to the flame of my adoration of the Mother (*matribhakti*). I took it as a marvellous chance and favourable condition for learning yoga and rising above dualities. I was of the extremists, in whose view democracy and equality between the rich and the poor formed a chief ingredient of nationalism. I remembered that thinking it our duty to turn the theory into practice, we had travelled together, on our way to Surat, in the same third class. In the camp the leaders, instead of making separate arrangements, would sleep in the same room along with the others. Rich, poor, brahmins, businessmen, shudra, Bengali, Maratha, Punjabi, Gujarati, we all stayed, slept, ate together with a wonderful feeling of brotherhood. We slept on the ground, ate the normal fare, made of rice-pulse-curd, in every way it was superlatively *swadeshi*. The "foreign-returned" from Bombay and Calcutta and the brahmin-born Madrasi with his tilak (head-mark) had become one body. During my stay in the Alipore jail I ate, lived and went through the same hardship and enjoyed the same 'privileges' with the other convicts, my fellow nationals, peasants, iron-mongers, potters, the *dom*s and the *bagdi*s, and I could learn of the ways of the Lord who dwells in everybody, this socialism and unity, this sense of nation-wide brotherhood had put its stamp on my life's dedication (*jivan brata*). The day when, before the sacred altar of the World-Mother in the form of the Motherland, all the orders of the country will stand with proud heads as brothers and as of the same mind, thanks to the loving kindness of my fellow convicts and prisoners as well as the impartiality of the British administrators, during the imprisonment I could feel the coming of that happy day and many a time it brought such a delight and thrill. The other day I noticed that the *Indian Social Reformer*, from Poona, had ironically commented on one of my simple, easy-to-understand statements by remarking: "We find an excess of Godwardness in the prison!" Alas for the pride and littleness of men, seeking after renown, men of little learning, proud of their little virtues! The manifestation of God, should it not be in prisons, in huts, ashrams, in the hearts of the poor, instead of in the temples of luxury of the rich or the bed of repose of the pleasure-seeking selfish worldly folk? God does not look for learning, honour, leadership, popular acclaim, outward ease and sophistication. To the poor He reveals Himself in the form of the Compassionate Mother. He who sees the Lord in all men, in all nations, in his own land, in the miserable, the poor, the fallen and the sinner and offers his life in the service of the Lord, the Lord comes to such hearts. So it is that in a fallen nation ready to rise, in the solitary prison of the servants of the nation the nearness of God grows.

After the jailor had seen to the blankets and the plates and bowls and left, I began to watch, sitting on the blanket, the scene before me. This solitary confinement seemed to me much better than the lock-up at Lal Bazar. There the silence of the commodious hall seemed to deepen the silence. Here the walls of the room seemed to come closer, eager to embrace one, like the all-pervading Brahman. There one cannot even look at the sky through the high windows of the second-storey room, it becomes hard to imagine that there are in this world trees and plants, men, animals, birds and houses. Here, since the door to the courtyard remains open, by sitting near the bars one could see the open space and the movement of the prisoners. Alongside the courtyard wall stood a tree, its green foliage a sight for sore eyes. The sentry that used to parade before the 'six decree' rooms, his face and footsteps often appeared dear to me like the welcome steps of a friend. The prisoners in the neighbouring cowshed would take out, in front of the room, the cows for grazing. Both cow and cowherd were daily and delightful sights. The solitary confinement at Alipore was a unique lesson in love. Before coming here even among people my affections had been confined to a rather narrow circle, and the closed emotions would rarely include birds and animals. I remember reading a poem by Rabibabu in which he describes, beautifully, a village boy's deep love for a buffalo. I did not at all understand it when I read it first. I had felt a note of exaggeration and artificiality in that description. Had I read that poem now, I would have seen it with other eyes. At Alipore I could feel how deep can be the love of man for all created things, how thrilled a man can be on seeing a cow, a bird, even an ant.

The first day in prison passed off peacefully. It was all so new as to be almost gay. Comparing it with the Lal Bazar lock-up I felt happy with my present circumstances, and since I had faith in God the loneliness did not weigh heavily on me. Even the strange spectacle of prison diet failed to disturb my attitude — coarse rice, even that spiced with husk, pebbles, insects, hair, dirt and such other stuff; tasteless lentil soup heavily watered; vegetables and greens mixed with grass and leaves. I never knew before that food could be so tasteless and without any nutritive value. Looking at its melancholy black visage I was appalled; and after two mouthfuls with a respectful salaam I took leave of it. All prisoners receive the same diet, and once a course gets going it goes on for ever. Then it was the Reign of Herbs. Days, fortnights and months passed by, but the same herbs (*shāk*), lentil and rice went on unchanged. What to speak of changing the menu, the preparation was not changed a jot or little; it was the same immutable, Eternal from beginning to end, a stable unique thing-in-itself. Within two evenings it was calculated to impress upon the prisoner the fragility of this world of maya. But even here I was luckier than the rest, this was because of the doctor's kindness. He had arranged a supply of milk from the hospital, thanks to which I had been spared on certain days from the vision of *shāk*.

That night I went to bed early, but it was no part of the prison regulations to be allowed to enjoy undisturbed sleep, since this might encourage a love of luxury among the prisoners. Hence there is a rule that every time

". . . since the door to the courtyard remains open, by sitting near the bars one could see the open space . . ."

sentries are changed, the prisoner has to be noisily disturbed and till he responds to their cries there is no respite. Among those who were engaged in this kind of patrolling the 'six decree' cells there were a few who would be no doubt remiss in their duty in this respect – among the police there was as a rule more of kindness and sympathy than strict sense of responsibility – this was especially so with the Hindustani policemen. Some of course remained obstinate. Waking us up at odd hours they would solitiously inquire about our well-being: "How do you do, Sir?" This untimely humour was not always pleasant or welcome, but I could see that they were but carrying out orders. For a few days in spite of the annoyance I put up with this show. In the end to preserve my sleep I had to scold them. Afterwards I noticed that this custom of seeking news about my well-being stopped of itself.

Next morning at four-fifteen the prison bell rang, this was the first bell to wake up the prisoners. There is a bell again after sometime, when the prisoners have to come out in file; after washing they have to swallow the prison gruel (*lufsi*) before starting the day's work. Knowing that it was impossible to sleep with the bells ringing every now and then, I also got up. The bars were removed at five, and after washing I sat inside the room once again. A little later *lufsi* was served at my doorstep; that day I did not take it but had only a vision of what it looked like. It was after a few days that I had the first taste of the 'great dish'. *Lufsi*, boiled rice, along with water, is the prisoner's little breakfast. A trinity, it takes three forms. On the first day it was *lufsi* in its Wisdom aspect, unmixed, original element, pure, white Shiva. On the second, it was the Hiranyagarbha aspect, boiled along with lentils, called *khichuri*, a yellowish medley. On the third day *lufsi* appeared in its aspect of Virat, a little mixed with jaggery, grey, slightly more fit for human consumption. I had thought the Wisdom and the Hiranyagarbha aspects to be beyond the capacity of average humanity and therefore made no efforts in that direction, but once in a while I had forced some of the Virat stuff within my system and marvelled, in delightful muse, about the many-splendoured virtues of British rule and the high level of western humanitarianism. It should be added that *lufsi* was the only nutritious diet for the Bengali prisoners, the rest were without any food value. But what of that? It had a taste, and one could eat this only out of sheer hunger; even then, one had to force and argue with oneself to be able to consume that stuff.

That day I took my bath at half-past eleven. For the first four or five days I had to keep wearing the same clothes in which I had come from home. At the time of bathing the old prisoner-warder from the cowshed, who had been appointed to look after me, managed to procure a piece of coarse cloth, a yard and half long, and till my only clothes did not dry I had to keep wearing this. I did not have to wash my clothes or dishes; a prisoner working in the cowshed would do that for me. Lunch was at eleven. To avoid the neighbourhood of the 'basket', and during the summer heat, I would often eat in the courtyard. The sentries did not object to this. The evening meal would be between five and five-thirty. From then on the door was not permitted to be opened. At seven rang the evening bell. The chief supervisor gathered the prison-warders together and loudly called out the names of the inmates, after which they would return to their respective posts. The tired prisoner then takes the refuge of sleep and in that has his only pleasure. It is the time when the weak of heart weeps over his misfortune or in anticipation of the hardships of prison life. And the lover of God feels the nearness of his deity, and has the joy of his prayer or meditation in the silent night. Then to these three thousand creatures who came from God, victims of a miserable social system, that huge instrument of torture, the Alipore jail, is lost in a vast Silence.

I would rarely meet the co-accused, who had been kept elsewhere. Behind the "six decrees" there were two rows of cells, making forty-four cells in all, the reason why it was known as forty-four decrees. Most of the accused were placed in one of these lines. Confined to the cells as they were, they did not suffer from solitary imprisonment, since there were three in each room. On the other side of the prison there was another decree, with a few large rooms. These could accommodate even upto twelve persons. Those who were fortunate enough to be placed in this decree lived more happily. Many were confined to a room in this decree, with leisure to talk day and night and spend their time happily in human companionship. But there was one who was deprived of this pleasure. This was Hemchandra Das. I do not know why the authorities were especially afraid of or angry with him. Out of so many people he had been singled out for solitary confinement. Hemchandra himself believed that since, in spite of much effort, the police had failed to make him admit his guilt, it explained their wrath. He was confined to a small room in the decree of which even the door would be closed from outside. I have said that this was the extreme form or type of punishment. From time to time the police would bring forward witnesses of different kind, colour and shape and enact the farce of an identification parade. On these occasions we would be made to line up, a long row, in front of the office. The prison authorities would mix up those accused on other charges along with us. But this was only in name. There was such obvious disparity between the two types of the accused; on the one hand the sharp, intelligent features of those involved in the bomb conspiracy; on the other hand, the soiled dress and lustreless visage of the average accused. If looking at them one could not make out the difference, that could only mean that one was a big fool, bereft of the lowest human intelligence. The prisoners were not however averse to the identification parade. It brought a kind of variety in prison life and provided a chance to exchange a few words. After our arrest it was during one of the parades that I could first meet my brother, Barindra, though we did not speak at that time. It was Narendranath Gossain who would often stand by my side, so I had a little more exchange with him. Extremely handsome, tall, strong, plump, but the eyes spoke of his evil propensities, nor did his words reveal any signs of intelligence. In this respect he was quite different from the other younger people. On their lips were often expressed high and pure ideas and their speech showed keen intelligence, above all, knowledge and noble selfless aspirations. But though Gossain's words were those of a fool and a light-hearted person, they expressed vigour and boldness. At that time he fully believed that he would be acquitted. He would say: "My

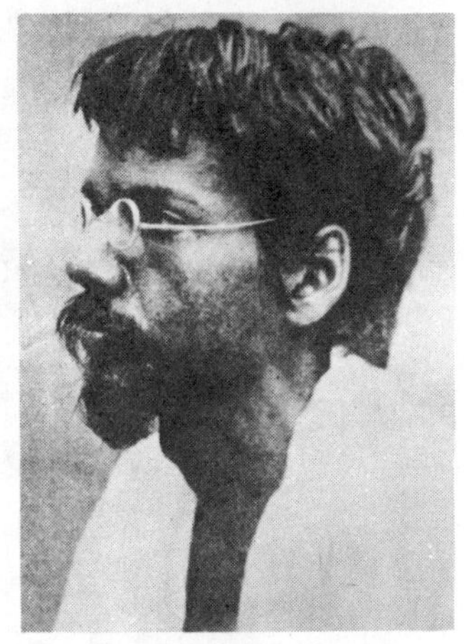

Barin K. Ghose

Upendranath Bannerjee

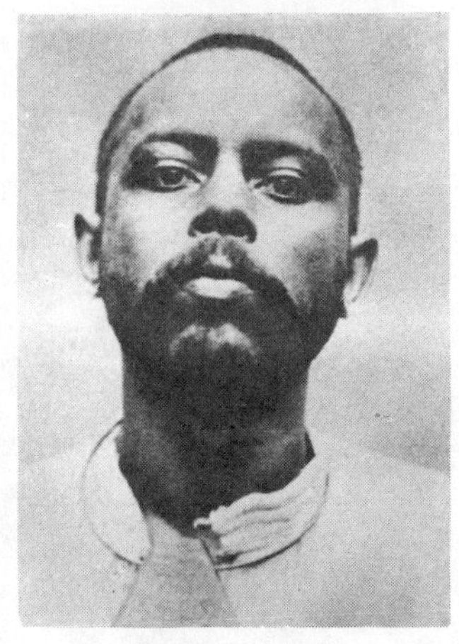

Ullaskar Dutt

Hemchandra Das

father is an expert in litigations; there the police can never beat him. My evidence too will not go against me for it will be proved that the police had got those statements by torturing me." I asked him, "You have sided with the police. Where are your witnesses?" Gossain answered unabashed: "My father has conducted hundreds of such cases; he knows this game very well. There will be no lack of witnesses." Of such stuff are approvers made.

Earlier we have referred to many of the needless sufferings and difficulties of the accused, but it should also be added that these were all part of prison administration; the sufferings were not due to any one's personal cruelty or lack of human qualities. Indeed, the persons on whom rested the administration of the Alipore Jail were all exceedingly polite, kindly and conscientious. If in any prison the prisoners' suffering has been lessened, and the inhuman barbarity of the western prison system lightened through kindness and conscientiousness, then that good out of evil has happened in the Alipore Jail under Mr. Emerson. This has happened due to two main reasons: the extraordinary qualities of its Superintendent, Mr. Emerson, and the assistant doctor, Baidyanath Chatterji. One of them was an embodiment of Europe's nearly vanished Christian ideals, the other was a personification of the charity and philanthropy that form the essence of Hinduism. Men like Mr. Emerson do not come to this country often, they are getting rare even in the West. In him could be found all the virtues of a Christian gentleman. Peace-loving, just, incomparably generous, full of rectitude, simple, straight and disciplined even towards inferiors, he was by nature incapable of anything but polite conduct. Among his shortcomings were lack of energy and administrative efficiency, he would leave all the responsibility to the jailor, himself remaining an idler. I do not think this caused much harm. The jailor, Jogendrababu, was a capable and efficient person, and, in spite of being seriously handicapped by diabetes, he would himself look after all the activities and since he was familiar with the boss's nature, he would respect justice and the absence of cruelty in the administration. Still he was not a great soul like Emerson, but only a minor Bengali officer; he knew how to keep the sahib in humour, would do his job efficiently and dutifully, treat others quietly and with natural politeness. Other than these I did not observe in him any other special quality. He had a great weakness for the service. More so since it was then the month of May and the time for his pension had drawn near, he was looking forward to well-earned rest from January next. The sudden appearance of the accused in the Alipore Bomb Conspiracy had caused in our jailor much fear and apprehension. There was no knowing what these violent energetic Bengali boys might be up to one of these days! The thought gave him no rest. He would say there was only an inch and half left for him to climb to the top of the palm tree. But he had succeeded in negotiating only half of that distance. Towards the end of August, Mr. Buchanan was pleased with his prison inspection. The jailor said gleefully, "This is Sahib's last visit during my term of office, there is nothing to worry about the pension now." Alas, for human blindness! The poet has truly said, God has given two great aids to the suffering race of man. First, he has covered the future with darkness; secondly, as man's sole support and consolation, he has endowed him with blind hope. Within five days of this statement by the jailor Naren Gossain fell a victim at the hands of Kanai, and Buchanan's visits to the prison grew increasingly frequent. The result was that Jogenbabu lost his job before time, and, because of the combined attack of sorrow and disease, he soon breathed his last. If instead of delegating all the work to such a subordinate, Emerson himself had looked after the administration, there would have been the possibility of greater improvement and reform during his regime. The little that he himself looked after was no doubt done properly; it was due to his character that the prison had become a place only for severe punishment and not turned into a veritable hell. Even after he had been transferred, the effect of his good work did not wholly disappear. Even now his successors have been obliged to keep sixty per cent of his humane measures intact.

Just as in the other jail departments Jogenbabu, a Bengali, was the chief, similarly in the hospital the Bengali doctor, Baidyanathbabu, was all-in-all. His superior officer, Doctor Daly, though not as charitable as Mr. Emerson, was out and out a gentleman and a most judicious person. He had high praise for the quiet demeanour, cheerfulness and sense of obedience of the boys, and loved to exchange pleasantries with younger people and also discuss with the other accused problems of religion, politics and philosophy. The doctor was of Irish stock and had inherited many of the qualities of that liberal and sentimental race. There was no meanness or duplicity about him; once in a while, when angry, he might use a rough word or behave harshly, but on the whole he loved to help people. He was familiar with the trickeries and the phoney diseases resorted to by the prisoners but sometimes, suspecting trickery, he would neglect even genuine sufferers. But once sure of the disease, he would prescribe with great care and kindness. Once I had a little temperature. It was then the rainy season; in the hospital's many-windowed huge verandah the moisture-laden wind played about freely, and yet I was unwilling either to go to the hospital or take medicine. My views on illness and cure had undergone change and I did not have much faith in medicines. Unless the disease was severe, nature herself would cure it in her own way, such was my belief. By yogically controlling the harm done by the humid air, I wished to verify and prove to the logical mind the success of my yogic training and methods. But the doctor was extremely anxious on my account, he explained to me with much eagerness the need to go to the hospital. And when I had gone there he looked after me with *empressement* and saw that I had meals such as I might get at home. Fearing that by staying in the prison wards my health might suffer, during the rains he desired that I should be comfortably lodged in the hospital. But I refused to stay longer in the hospital and insisted on going back to the ward. He was not equally considerate to everybody, especially those who were strong and healthy. He was afraid of keeping such people in the hospital even when they were sick. He had a false notion that if ever any incident took place it would be because of these strong and restless lads. What happened in the end was its exact opposite, the incident in the hospital was due to the ailing, emaciated Satyendranath Bose and the sick, quiet-natured Kanailal, a man of few words. Though Dr. Daly had his qualities, most of his good deeds were inspired and set in motion by Baidyanathbabu. I had never seen such a sympathetic soul before, nor do I expect to see it after; it was as if he had been born to help and do good to others. Whenever he heard of a case of suffering, to try to lessen it had become for him almost a natural and inevitable act. To the residents of this abode of misery, full of suffering, it was as if he was there to distribute the carefully collected celestial waters of bliss to these creatures of hell. The best way to remove any want, injustice or needless suffering was to see that a report of it reached the doctor's ears. If its removal lay within his powers he would never rest without doing it. Baidyanathbabu harboured in his heart a deep love of the motherland, but as a government servant he was unable to express that emotion. His only failing was his excessive sympathy. Though in a prison administrator this may be looked upon as a defect, in terms of higher ethics this may be described as the finest expression of one's humanity and the quality most beloved of God. He did not discriminate between the ordinary prisoners and the *'Bandemataram'* convicts; whoever was sick, or ailing, he kept them in the hospital with the same care and would be unwilling to let them go till they had wholly come round. It was this fault of his that was the real reason for his loss of job. After the killing of Gossain the authorities suspected his attitude and wrongfully dismissed him.

There is a special need to speak of the kindness and human conduct of these officers. The prison arrangements made for our detention I have been obliged to describe earlier, and afterwards too I shall try to show the inhuman cruelty of the British prison system. Lest some readers look upon this cruelty as an evil effect of these officers, I have described the qualities of some of the chiefs of the staff. In the description of the early stages of prison life there will be some further evidence of these qualities.

I have described my mental state on the first day of solitary confinement. For a few days I had to go without books or any other aid to spend the period of forced isolation. Later on Mr. Emerson came and handed over to me the permission to get some clothes and reading material from home. After procuring from the prison authorities pen and ink, and their official stationery, I wrote to my respected maternal uncle, the well-known editor of *Sanjibani*, to send my *dhoti* and *kurta*; among books I asked for the Gita and the Upanishads. It took a couple of days for the books to reach me. Before that I had enough leisure to realise the enormity or dangerous potentiality of solitary confinement. I could understand why even firm and well-developed intellects break down in such a state of confinement and readily turn towards insanity. At the same time, I could realise God's infinite mercy and the rare advantage offered by these same conditions. Before imprisonment I was in the habit of sitting down for meditation for an hour in the morning and evening. In this solitary prison, not having anything else to do, I tried to meditate for a longer period. But for those unaccustomed it is not easy to control and steady the mind pulled in a thousand directions. Somehow I was able to concentrate for an hour and half or two, later the mind rebelled while the body too was fatigued. At first the mind was full of thoughts of many kinds. Afterwards, devoid of human conversation and an insufferable listlessness due to absence of any subject of thought, the mind gradually lost its capacity to think. There was for a time a condition when it seemed a thousand indistinct ideas were hovering round the doors of the mind but with the gates closed; one or two that were able to get through were frightened by the silence of these mental states and quietly ran away. In this uncertain, dull state I suffered an intense mental agony. In the hope of mental solace and rest for the overheated brain I looked at the beauties of nature outside, but with that solitary tree, a sliced sky and the cheerless prospects in the prison how long can the mind, in such a state, find consolation? I looked towards the blank wall. Gazing at the lifeless white surface the mind seemed to grow even more hopeless; realising the agony of the imprisoned condition, the brain was restless. I again sat down to meditate. It was impossible. The intense baffled attempt made the mind only more tired, useless, made it burn and boil. I looked around, at last I found some large black ants moving about a hole in the ground, and I spent some time watching their efforts and movements. Later I noticed some tiny red ants. Soon there was a big battle between the black and the red, the black ants began to bite and kill the red ants. I felt an intense charity and sympathy for those unjustly treated red ants and tried to save them from the black killers. This gave me an occupation and something to think about. Thanks to the ants I passed a few days like this. Still there was no way to spend the long days ahead. I tried to argue with myself, did some deliberate reflection, but day after day the mind rebelled and felt increasingly desolate. It was as though time weighed heavy, an unbearable torture; broken by that pressure it did not have leisure even to breathe freely. It was like being throttled by an enemy in a dream and yet without the strength to move one's limbs. I was amazed at this condition! True, while outside, I never wished to stay idle or without any activity, still I have spent long periods in solitary musings. Had the mind now become so weak that the solitude of a few days could make me so restless? Perhaps, I thought, there is a world of difference between voluntary and compulsory solitude. It is one thing to stay alone in one's home, but to have to stay, forced by others, in a solitary prison cell is quite another. There one can turn at will to men for refuge, find shelter in book knowledge and its stylistic elegance, in the dear voice of friends, the noise on the roadside, in the varied shows of the world, one can find joy of mind and feel at ease. But here, bound to the wheels of an iron law, subservient to the whim of others, one had to live deprived of every other contact. According to the proverb, one who can stand solitude is either a god or a brute, it is a discipline quite beyond the power of men. Previously I was unable to believe in what the proverb said, now I could feel that even for one accustomed to the yogic life this discipline is not easy to acquire. I remember the terrifying end of the Italian regicide, Breci. His cruel judges, instead of ordering him to be hanged, had given him seven years' solitary imprisonment. Within a year Breci had gone mad. But he had endured for some time! Was my mental strength so poor? Then I did not know that God was having a game with me, through which He was giving me a few necessary lessons. First, He showed me the state of mind in which prisoners condemned to solitary cells move towards insanity, and turned me wholly against the inhuman cruelty of the western prison administration, so that I might, to the best of my ability, turn my countrymen and the world from these barbarous ways to the path of more humane prison organisation. This was the first lesson. I remembered, fifteen years back, after return home from England, I had written some bitterly critical articles in the *Induprakash*, of Bombay, against the petitionary ethics of the then Congress. Seeing that these articles were influencing the minds of the young, the late Mahadeo Govind Ranade had told me, when I met him, for nearly half an hour, that I should give up writing these articles, and advised me to take up some other Congress work. He was desirous of my taking up the work of prison reform. I was astonished and unhappy at the unexpected suggestion and had refused to undertake that work. I did not know then that this was a prelude to the distant future and that one day God himself would keep me in prison for a year and make me see the cruelty and futility of the system and the need for reform. Now I understand that in the present political atmosphere there was no possibility of any reform of the prison system, but I resolved before my conscience to propagate and argue in its favour so that these hellish remnants of an alien order were not perpetuated in a self-determining India. I also understood His second purpose: it was to reveal and expose before my mind its own weakness so that I might get rid of it for ever. For one who seeks the yogic state, crowd and solitude should mean the same. Indeed, the weakness dropped off within a very few days, and now it seems that the mental poise would not be disturbed even by twenty years of solitude. In the dispensation of the All-Good (*mangalmaya*) even out of evil cometh good. The third purpose was to give me this lesson that my yoga practices would not be done by personal effort, but that a spirit of faith or reverence (*sraddha*) and complete self-surrender (*atma-samarpana*) were the road to attain perfection in yoga, and whatever power or realisation the Lord would give out of His benignity, to accept and utilise these should be the only aim of my yogic endeavour. Since the day when the deep darkness of Ignorance began to lessen, I started to see the true nature of the All-Good Lord's amazing infinite goodness as I watched the different events in the ward. There is no event – great or small or even the smallest – from which some good has not accrued. He often fulfils three or four aims through a single event. We frequently see the working of a blind force in the world; accepting waste as part of nature's method we ignore God's omniscience and find fault with the divine Intelligence. The charge is unfounded. The divine Intelligence never works blindly, there cannot be the slightest waste of His power, rather the restrained manner in which, through the minimum of means, He achieves a variety of results is beyond the human intelligence.

Troubled by mental listlessness I spent a few days in agony in this manner. One afternoon as I was thinking, streams of thought began to flow endlessly and then suddenly these grew so uncontrolled and incoherent that

I could feel that the mind's regulating power was about to cease. Afterwards when I came back to myself, I could recollect that though the power of mental control had ceased, the intelligence was not self-lost or did not deviate for a moment, but it was as if the intelligence was watching quietly this marvellous phenomenon. But at that time, shaking with the terror of being overcome by insanity, I had not been able to notice that. I called upon God with eagerness and intensity and prayed to him to prevent my loss of intelligence. That very moment there spread over my being such a gentle and cooling breeze, the heated brain became relaxed, easy and supremely blissful such as in all my life I had never known before. Just as a child sleeps, secure and without fear, on the lap of his mother, so I remained on the lap of the World-Mother. From that day all my trouble of prison life were over. Afterwards on many occasions, during the period of detention, inquietude, solitary imprisonment, and mental unease because of lack of activity, bodily trouble or disease, in the lean periods of yogic life, these have come, but that day in a single moment God had given my inner being such strength that these sorrows as they came and went did not leave any trace or touch on the mind; relishing strength and delight in the sorrow itself the mind was able to reject these subjective sufferings. The sufferings seemed as fragile as water drops on a lotus leaf. Then when the books came, their need had considerably lessened. I could have stayed on even if the books were not there. Though it is not the purpose of these articles to write a history of my inner life, still I could not but mention this fact. From this one incident it will be clear how it was possible to live happily during long solitary confinement. It was for this reason that God had brought about this situation or experience. Without turning me mad he had enacted in my mind the gradual process towards insanity that takes place in solitary confinement, keeping my intelligence as the unmoved spectator of the entire drama. Out of this came strength, and I had an excess of kindness and sympathy for the victims of human cruelty and torture. I also realised the extraordinary power and efficacy of prayer.

During the period of my solitary confinement Dr. Daly and the Assistant Superintendent would come to my room almost every day and have a little chat. From the beginning, I do not know why I had been able to draw their special favour and sympathy. I did not speak much with them, but just answered only when they specifically asked something. If they raised any issue I either listened quietly or would stop after speaking a few words. Yet they did not give up visiting me. One day Dr. Daly spoke to me, "I have been able, through my Assistant Superintendent, to get the big boss to agree that every day, in the morning and evening, you will be allowed to take a walk in front of the decree. I do not like that you should be confined throughout the day in a small cell, it's bad for both body and mind." From that day on I would take a stroll every day in the morning and evening in the open space before the decree. In the afternoons it would be for ten, fifteen or twenty minutes, in the morning for an hour; at times I would stay out for two hours, there was no time limit about it. I enjoyed this very much. On one side were the jail industries, on the other the cowshed – my independent kingdom was flanked by these two. From

Sri Aurobindo (1908-09)

the industrial section to the cowshed, from the cowshed to industrial section, travelling to and fro I would recite the deeply moving, ageless, powerful *mantras* of the Upanishads, or watching the movements and activities of the prisoners I tried to realise the basic truths of the immanent Godhead, God in every form. In the trees, the houses, the walls, in men, animals, birds, metals, the earth, with the help of the *mantra*: All this is the Brahman (*sarvam khalvidam Brahma*). I would try to fix or impose that realisation on all of these. As I went on doing like this sometimes the prison ceased to appear to be a prison at all. The high wall, those iron bars, the white wall, the green-leaved tree shining in sunlight, it seemed as if these commonplace objects were not unconscious at all, but that they were vibrating with a universal consciousness, they loved me and wished to embrace me, or so I felt. Men, cows, ants, birds are moving, flying, singing, speaking, yet all is Nature's play; behind all this is a great pure detached Spirit rapt in a serene delight. Once in a while it seemed as if God Himself was standing under the tree, to play upon his Flute of Delight, and with its sheer charm to draw my very soul out. Always it seemed as if someone was embracing me, holding me on his lap. The manifestation of these emotions overpowered my whole body and mind, a pure and wide peace reigned everywhere. It is impossible to describe that. The hard cover of my life opened up and a spring of love for all creatures gushed from within. Along with this love such *sattwic* emotions as charity, kindness, *ahimsa*, etc., overpowered my dominantly *rajasic* nature and found an abundant release. And the more these qualities developed, the greater the delight and the deeper the sense of unclouded peace. The anxiety over the case had vanished from the beginning, now it was a contrary emotion that found room in my mind. God is All-Good, he had brought me into the prison house for my good, my release and the quashing of the charge was certain, I grew firm in this faith. After this for many days I did not have to suffer any troubles in the jail.

It took some days for these emotions to settle and deepen. It was while this was going on that the case opened in the magistrate's court. At first the mind was greatly perturbed at being dragged from the silence of solitary confinement to the noise of the world outside. The patience of inner discipline was lost and the mind did not at all consent to listen for five hours on end to the dull and bothersome arguments by the prosecution. At first I tried to continue the inner life while sitting in the court-room, but the unaccustomed mind would be attracted to every sound, sight, and the attempt would not succeed. Later the feelings changed and I acquired the power to reject from the mind the immediate sounds and sights, and draw the mind inwards. But this did not take place in the early stages, the true power of concentration had not developed then. For that reason, giving up the futile attempt, I would be content with seeing, now and then, God in all creatures; for the rest I would observe the words and behaviour of my companions in adversity, else think of other things, or sometimes listen to Mr. Norton's valuable remarks or even to the evidence of witnesses. I found that while spending one's time in solitary imprisonment had grown easy and pleasant, it was not that easy in the midst of the crowd and in the life-and-death game of a serious political case. I greatly enjoyed the laughter and the pleasantries of the accused lads; else the time spent at the court appeared wholly annoying. At four-thirty I would happily get into the police van and return to the prison.

The contact of human life and each other's company, after fifteen or sixteen days of jail life, made the other prisoners extremely happy. As soon as they got into the carriage the fountain of laughter and conversation would open and during the ten minutes that they were inside the carriage the stream would never cease for a moment. On the first day they took us to the court with great pomp. There was a small platoon of European sergeants who went along with us and they all carried loaded pistols. At the time of our getting into the carriage a band of armed policemen stood guard round us and did some marching behind the carriage; the ritual was repeated at the time of our getting down as well. Looking at so much to-do the inexperienced spectator might have thought these laughter-loving young lads must be some group of dare-devil famous warriors. Who knows how much courage and strength resided in their bodies so that even with their empty hands they might be able to break through the impassive cordon of a hundred policemen and tommies! May be it was for this reason that we were being conducted with such honour and ceremony. For a few days the pomp was kept up, then there was a gradual decline; in the end two to four sergeants would be there to fetch and bring us back. At the time of our getting down they did not really very much observe how we entered the prison; we would walk into it as if we were returning home after a stroll, just as a free person does. Watching this carelessness and slackening of duties the

Police Commissioner and some of the Superintendents said angrily: "On the first day we had arranged for twenty-five to thirty sergeants, now we see that not even four or five turn up." They would scold the sergeants and make strict arrangements for supervision. Then, maybe for two days, two more sergeants would come, and again the earlier slackness followed! The sergeants found that the devotees of the bomb were quite harmless folk, who were also not attempting to escape and had no plans to kill or attack anyone, so they wondered why they should waste valuable time in performing unpleasant duties. At first before entering and leaving the court there used to be a personal search, during which we used to have the joy of feeling the soft palms of the sergeants; otherwise one was not likely to gain or lose from this search. It was clear that our protectors had profound scepticism about the utility of such a procedure, and after a few days this was also given up. We could safely carry with us into the courtroom books, bread and sugar just as we liked. They soon lost the feeling that we were there to hurl a bomb or fire a pistol. But I noticed that there was one singular fear from which the sergeant's mind was not free. Who knew which of the accused would have the evil brainwave of hurling a pair of shoes at the glorious pate of the magistrate? Then the fat would be in the fire. For this reason entering the court with shoes on was strictly forbidden, and the sergeants were always alert on that point. I did not notice them to be keen on any other safety measures.

The nature of the case was a little strange. Magistrate, counsel, witnesses, evidence, exhibits, accused, all appeared strange. Watching, day after day, the endless stream of witnesses and exhibits, the counsel's unvaried dramatic performance, the boyish frivolity and light-heartedness of the youthful magistrate, looking at the amazing spectacle I often thought that instead of sitting in a British court of justice we were inside a stage in some world of fiction. Let me describe some of the odd inhabitants of that kingdom.

The star performer of the show was the government counsel, Mr. Norton. Not only the star performer, but he was also its composer, stage manager and prompter – a versatile genius like him must be rare in the world. Counsel Mr. Norton hailed from Madras, hence it appeared he was unaccustomed and inexperienced in the common code and courtesy as it obtained among the barristers of Bengal. He had been at one time a leader of the National Organisation, and for that reason might have been incapable of tolerating opposition and contradiction, and was in the habit of punishing opponents. Such natures are known to be ferocious. I cannot say whether Mr. Norton had been the lion of Madras Corporation, but he certainly was the king among the beasts at the Alipore Court. It was hard to admire his depth of legal acumen – which was as rare as winter in summer. But in the ceaseless flow of words and, through verbal quips, in the strange ability to transmute an inconsequential witness into something serious, in the brashness of making wild statements with little or no ground, in riding roughshod over witnesses and junior barristers and in the charming ability to turn white into black, to see his incomparable genius in action was but to admire him. Among the great counsels there are three kinds – those who, through their legal acumen, satisfactory exposition and subtle analysis, can create a favourable impression on the judge; those who can skilfully draw out the truth from the witnesses and presenting the facts of the case and the subject under discussion draw the mind of the judge or the jury towards themselves; and those who, through their loud speech, by threats and oratorical flow can dumbfound the witness and splendidly confuse the entire issue, and win the case by distracting the intelligence of the judge or the jury. Mr. Norton is foremost in this third category. This is by no means to be counted as a defect. The counsel is a worldly person, he takes money for his service, to gain the intention of the client is his duty – that is what he is there for. Now, according to the British legal system, the bringing out of truth by the contending parties, complainant and defendant, is not the real purpose; to win the case, by hook or by crook, is what it is really after. Hence the counsel must bend his energies towards that end, else he would be unfaithful to the law of his being. If God has not endowed one with other qualities, then one must fight with such qualities as one possesses, and win the case with their help. Thus Mr. Norton was but following the law of his own being (*swadharma*). The government paid him a thousand rupees a day. In case this turned out to be a useless expenditure the government would be a loser. Mr. Norton was trying heart and soul to prevent such a loss to the government. But in a political case, the accused have to be given wide privileges and not to emphasise doubtful or uncertain evidence were rules germane to the British legal system. Had Mr. Norton cared to remember this convention it

Prosecution Counsel Eardley Norton

would not have, I feel, harmed the case. On the other hand, a few innocent persons would have been spared the torture of solitary imprisonment and innocent Ashok Nandi might have even been alive. The counsel's leonine nature was probably at the root of the trouble. Just as Holinshed and Plutarch had collected the material for Shakespeare's historical plays, in the same manner the police had collected the material for this drama of a case. And Mr. Norton happened to be the Shakespeare of this play. I, however, noticed a difference between Shakespeare and Mr. Norton: Shakespeare would now and then leave out some of the available material, but Mr. Norton never allowed any material, true or false, cogent or irrelevant, from the smallest to the largest, to go unused; on top of it he could weave such a wonderful plot by his self-created and abundant suggestion, inference and hypothesis that the great poets and writers of fiction like Shakespeare and Defoe would have to acknowledge defeat before this grand master of the art. The critic might say that just as Falstaff's hotel bill showed a pennyworth of bread and countless gallons of wine, similarly in Norton's plot an ounce of proof was mixed with tons of inference and suggestion. But even detractors are bound to praise the elegance and construction of the plot. It gave me great happiness that Mr. Norton had chosen me as the protagonist of this play. Like Satan in Milton's *Paradise Lost*, in Mr. Norton's plot at the centre of the mighty rebellion stood I, an extraordinarily sharp, intelligent and powerful, bold, bad man! Of the national movement I was the alpha and the omega, its creator and saviour, engaged in undermining the British empire. As soon as he came across any piece of excellent or vigorous writing in English he would jump and loudly proclaim, Aurobindo Ghose! All the legal and illegal, the organised activities or unexpected consequences of the movement were the doings of Aurobindo Ghose! and when they are the doings of Aurobindo Ghose then, even when lawfully admissible, they must contain hidden illegal intentions and potentialities. He probably thought that if I were not caught within two years, it would be all up with the British empire. If my name ever appeared on any torn sheet of paper, Mr. Norton's joy knew no bounds. With great cordiality he would present it at the holy feet of the presiding magistrate. It is a pity I was not born as an Avatar; otherwise, thanks to his intense devotion and ceaseless contemplation of me for the nonce, he would surely have earned his release, *mukti*, then and there and both the period of our detention and the government's expenses would have been curtailed. Since the sessions court declared me innocent of the charges, Norton's plot was sadly shorn of its glory and elegance. By leaving the Prince of Denmark out of *Hamlet* the humourless judge, Beachcroft, damaged the greatest poem of the twentieth century. If the critic is allowed his right to alter poetic compositions, such loss of meaning can hardly be prevented. Norton's other agony was that some of the witnesses too seemed so cussed that they had wholly refused to bear evidence in keeping with his fabricated plot. At this Norton would grow red with fury and, roaring like a lion, he would strike terror in the heart of the witness and cower him down. Like the legitimate and irrepressible anger of a poet when his words are altered, or of a stage manager when the actor's declamation, tone or postures go against his directions, Norton felt a comparable loss of temper. His quarrel with barrister Bhuban Chatterji had this holy or *sattwic* anger as its root. Such an inordinately insensitive person as Mr. Chatterji I have not come across. He had no sense of time or propriety. For instance, whenever Mr. Norton sacrificed the distinction between the relevant and the irrelevant, or tried to force odd arguments purely for the sake of poetic effect, Mr. Chatterji would invariably get up and raise objections and declare these as inadmissible. He did not appreciate that these were being furnished not because they were relevant or legal, but because they might serve the purpose of Norton's stage-craft. At such impropriety not Norton alone but Mr. Birley could hardly contain himself. Once Mr. Birley addressed Chatterji in a pathetic tone: "Mr. Chatterji, we were getting on very nicely before you came." Indeed so, if one raises objections at every word the drama does not proceed, nor has the audience the joy of it.

If Mr. Norton was the author of the play, its protagonist and stage manager, Mr. Birley may well be described as its patron. He seemed to be a credit to his Scotch origin. His figure was a symbol or reminder of Scotland. Very fair, quite tall, extremely spare, the little head on the long body seemed like little Ochterlonie sitting on top of the sky-kissing Ochterlonie monument, or as if a ripe coconut had been put on the crest of Cleopatra's obelisk! Sandy-haired, all the cold and ice of Scotland seemed to lie frozen on his face. So tall a person needed an intelligence to match, else one had to be sceptical about the economy of nature. But in this matter of the creation of Birley, probably the Creatrix had been slightly unmindful and inattentive. The English poet

Marlowe has described this frugality as "infinite riches in a little room" but encountering Mr. Birley one has an opposite feeling, of little riches in an infinite room. Finding so little intelligence in such a tallish body one indeed felt pity. Remembering how a few such administrators were governing thirty crores of Indians could not but rouse a deep devotion towards the majesty of the English masters and their methods of administration. Mr. Birley's knowledge of law came a cropper during the cross-examination by Srijut Byomkesh Chakravarty. Asked to declare when he had taken charge of the case in his own benign hands and how to complete the process of taking over charge of a case, after years of magistracy Mr. Birley's head reeled to find these out. Unable to solve the problem he finally tried to save his skin by leaving it to Mr. Chakravarty to decide. Even now among the most complex problems of the case the question remains as to when Mr. Birley had taken over this case. The pathetic appeal to Mr. Chatterji, which I have quoted earlier, will help one to infer Mr. Birley's manner of judgment. From the start, charmed by Mr. Norton's learning and rhetoric, he had been completely under his spell. He would follow, ever so humbly, the road pointed out by Norton. Agreeing with his views, he laughed when Norton laughed, grew angry as Norton would be angry. Looking at this daft, childlike conduct one sometimes felt tenderly and paternally towards him. Birley was exceedingly childlike. I could never think of him as a magistrate, it seemed as if a school student, suddenly turned teacher, was sitting at the teacher's high desk. That was the manner in which he conducted the affairs of the court. In case someone did not behave pleasantly towards him, he would scold him like a schoolmaster. If any one of us, bored with the farce of a case, started to talk among ourselves, Mr. Birley would snap like a schoolmaster; in case people did not obey he would order everybody to keep standing and if this was not done at once, he would tell the sentry to see to it. We had grown so accustomed to the schoolmasterish manner that when Birley and Chatterji had started to quarrel we were expecting every moment that the barrister would soon be served with the stand-up order. But Mr. Birley adopted an opposite course. Shouting "Sit down, Mr. Chatterji", he made this new and disobedient pupil of the Alipore School take his seat. Just as when a student asks questions or demands further explanation, an irritated teacher threatens him, so whenever the advocate representing the accused raised objections, Mr. Birley would threaten him. Some witnesses gave Norton a hell of a time. Norton wanted to prove that a particular piece of writing was in the handwriting of such-and-such accused. If the witness said: "No sir, this is not exactly like that handwriting, but may be, one cannot be sure" – many witnesses answered like that – Norton would become quite agitated. Scolding, shouting, threatening, he would try somehow to get the desired answer. And his last question would be, "What is your belief? Do you think it is so or not?" To this the witness could say neither "yes" nor "no". Every time, again and again, he would repeat the same answer and try to make Norton understand that he had no "belief" in the matter and was swayed between scepticisms. But Norton did not care for such an answer. Every time he would hurl back the same question, like thunder, at the witness: "Come, sir, what is your belief?" Mr. Birley, in his turn, would catch fire from the embers of Norton's anger, and thunder from his high seat above: "*Tomar biswas ki achhay*?"[1] Poor witness! he would be in a dilemma. He had no "biswas" (belief) at all, yet on one side of him was ranged the magistrate and, on the other, like a hungry tiger, Norton was raging in a circle to disembowel him and get at the priceless never-to-be-had "biswas". Often the "biswas" might not materialise and, his brain in a whirl, the sweating witness would escape with his life from the torture chamber. Some, who held their life dearer than their "biswas", would make good their escape by offering an artificial "biswas" at the feet of Mr. Norton, who, now of course highly pleased, would conduct the rest of the cross-examination with care and affability. Because such a counsel had been matched with a magistrate of the same calibre the case had all the more taken on the proportions of a play.

Though a few of the witnesses went against Mr. Norton, the majority provided answers in support of his leading questions. Among these there were few familiar faces. One or two we of course knew; of these Devdas Karan helped to dispel our boredom and made us hold our sides with laughter, for which we shall remain eternally grateful to him. In course of giving evidence he said that, at the time of the Midnapore Conference when Surendrababu had asked from his students devotion to the teacher, *gurubhakti*, Aurobindobabu had spoken out: "What did Drona do?" Hearing this Mr. Norton's eagerness and curiosity knew no bounds. He must have thought "Drona" to be a devotee of the bomb or a political

[1] What is your belief? Or, simply, What do you think?

killer or someone associated with the Manicktola Garden or the Student's Store. Mr Norton may have thought that the phrase meant that Aurobindo Ghose was advising the giving of bombs to Surendrababu as a reward instead of *gurubhakti,* for such an interpretation would have helped the case considerably. Hence he asked eagerly: "What did Drona do?"[1] At first the witness was unable to make out the nature of the [silly] question. And for five minutes a debate went on. In the end, throwing his hands high, Sri Karan told Norton: "Drona performed many a miracle." This did not satisfy Mr Norton. How could he be content without knowing the whereabouts of Drona's bomb? So he asked again: "What do you mean by that? Tell me what exactly he did." The witness gave many answers, but in none was Dronacharya's life's secret unravelled as Norton would have liked it. He now lost his temper and started to growl. The witness too began to shout. An advocate smilingly expressed the doubt that perhaps the witness did not know what Drona had done. At this Sri Karan went wild with anger and wounded pride, *abhiman*. "What", he shouted, "I, I do not know what Drona had done? Bah, have I read the *Mahabharata* from cover to cover in vain?" For half an hour a battle royal was waged between Norton and Karan over Drona's corpse. Every five minutes, shaking the Alipore Judge's Court, Norton hurled his question; "Out with it, Mr. Editor. What did Drona do?" In answer the editor began a long cock-and-bull story, but there was no reliable news about what Drona had done. The

[1] In the *Mahabharata*, Drona or Dronacharya is a preceptor of the royal princes. Norton and others, ignorant of the reference, took him to be a contemporary character, in fact a conspirator.

entire court reverberated with peals of laughter. At last, after the tiffin, Sri Karan came back after a little reflection with a cool head, and he suggested this solution of the problem, that poor Drona had done nothing and that the half-hour long tug of war over his departed soul had been in vain. It was Arjuna who had killed his *guru* Drona. Thanks to this false accusation, Dronacharya, relieved, must have offered his thanks at Kailasha to Sadashiva, that because of Sri Karan's evidence he did not have to stand in the dock in the Alipore Bomb Conspiracy Case. A word from the editor would have easily established his relationship with Aurobindo Ghose. But the all-merciful Sadashiva had saved him from such a calamity.

The witnesses in the case could be divided into three categories. There were the police and the secret service men; there were people from the lower classes and other gentry who, for misdeeds of their own, seemed to be deeply in love with the police; and there were others who, because of their own personal failings and being deprived of the love of the police, had been dragged unwillingly to give evidence. Each category had its own style of offering evidence. The gentlemen of the police would say their say, already decided upon, quite cheerfully, without hesitation, just as it pleased them; would recognise those they had to, without a shade of doubt, hesitation or any margin of error. The friends of the police would give witness with considerable alacrity; those they had to identify they would, but sometimes in their excessive eagerness they would identify even those who were not to be identified. Those who had been brought there against their wishes would say only what they knew, but this would come to very little and Norton would not be satisfied. Assuming that the witness was holding back highly valuable and certain proof, he would make every attempt to cross-examine him and get the secret out of his system by a surgical operation of the abdomen, as it were. This put the witness into a good deal of difficulty. On one side stood a thundering Mr. Norton, a red-eyed Mr. Birley, on the other a sense of the great sin of sending, on false evidence, one's countrymen to the Andaman Islands. Whether to please Norton and Birley or God, for the witness this question assumed serious proportions. On one side, there was temporary danger because of incurring other men's displeasure; on the other, hell and misery in the next life due to one's evil deeds. But the witness would reflect: hell and the next life are still far beyond while the man-made dangers might swallow him at the next moment. The fear that they might be convicted of bearing false evidence because of their unwillingness to do so was likely to be shared by many, since in such cases the consequences were none too rare. For this type of witness the time spent in the witness-box was made up of a mixture of fear and agony. At the end of the cross-examination their half-departed life would return to their bodies and relieve them of the suffering. Some, however, gave their evidence boldly without caring for Norton's rage, at which the English counsel, following national habit, would soften. Like this so many witnesses came and went and gave such a variety of evidence, but not one helped the police cause in any way worth mentioning. One of them spoke quite plainly, "I know nothing, and cannot understand why the police have dragged me into it!" This sort of method for conducting cases is possible perhaps only in India. Had it been some other country the judge would have been annoyed and would have severely censured and taught the police a lesson. Hauling hundreds of witnesses, gathered on a basis of guesswork and without inquiring whether one was guilty or not, wasting the country's finances and keeping without any sense the accused for long periods under the hardship of prison life, is worthy only of the police force of this country. But what were the poor police to do? They are detectives only in name, but without much of their own. Hence to throw a wide net and catch good, bad and indifferent witnesses in this manner and bring them to the witness box, like pigs in a poke, was their only way. Who knows, these men might have some information, even provide some proof.

The method for identification was also equally mysterious. First, the witness was asked, "Would you be able to recognise any one of these persons?" If the witness answered, "Yes, I can," the happy Mr. Norton would arrange for the identification parade in the witness box itself and order him to demonstrate the powers of his memory. In case the man said, "I am not sure, maybe I can recognise," Mr. Norton would grow a little sad and say, "All right, go and try." When someone said, "No, I can't, I haven't seen them" or, "I did not mark carefully," Mr. Norton would not let him go even then. Looking at so many faces some memory of the past life might come back, with that hope he would send him to the experiment to find out. The witness however lacked such a yogic power. Perhaps the fellow had no faith in the past life, and gravely marching, under the sergeant's supervision, between two long rows of accused persons, he would say, without even looking at us, "No, I don't know any one of them." Crestfallen, Norton would take back his human net without any catch. In course of this trial there was a marvellous illustration of how sharp and correct human memory could be. Thirty to forty people would be kept standing; one didn't know their name, hadn't known them at all in this or any other life, yet whether one had seen or not seen someone two months back, or seen such a person at three places and not seen in the other two, may be one had seen him brush his teeth once, and so his figure remained imprinted in the brain for all time. When did one see this person, what was he doing, was there anyone else with him, or was he alone? One remembers nothing of these, yet his figure is fixed in one's mind for all times; one has met Hari ten times, so there is no probability of forgetting him; but even if one has seen Shyam only for half a minute, one would not be able to forget him till one's last breath, and with no possibility of mistake, – such a prodigious power of memory is not to be found frequently in this imperfect human nature, this earth wrapped up in matter and its unconsciousness. But not one, not two, every police chap seemed to be the owner of such uncanny, error-proof accurate memory – for which our devotion and respect for the C.I.D. grew more profound day by day. It is not that in the magistrate's court we did not have, once or twice, occasions for scepticism. When I found in the written evidence that Sisir Ghose had been in Bombay in the month of April, yet a few police chaps had seen him precisely during that period in Scott's Lane and Harrison Road, one could not but feel a little uneasy. And when

Birendrachandra Sen, of Sylhet, while he was physically present at Baniachung, at his father's place, became visible in his subtle body to the occult vision of the C.I.D. at the Garden and Scott's Lane – of which Scott's Lane Birendra knew nothing, as was proved conclusively in the written evidence – the doubts could not but deepen, especially when those who had never set their feet in Scott's Lane were informed that the police had often found them there, in the circumstances a little suspicion seemed not unnatural. A witness from Midnapore – whom the accused persons from Midnapore however described as a secret service agent – said that he had seen Hemchandra Sen of Sylhet lecturing at Tamluk. Now Hemchandra had never seen Tamluk with his mortal eyes, yet his shadow-self had rushed from Sylhet to Midnapore and, with his powerful and seditionary nationalist speech he had delighted the eyes and ears of our respected detective. But the causal body of Charuchandra Roy of Chandernagore, materialising at Manicktola, had perpetrated even greater mysteries. Two police officers declared on oath that on such and such date at such and such time they had seen Charubabu at Shyambazar, from where he had walked, in the company of a conspirator, to the Manicktola Gardens. They had followed him there and watched him from close quarters, and there could be no ground for error. Both witnesses did not budge when cross examined. The words of Vyasa are true indeed – *vyasasya vachanam satyam*. The evidence of the police also cannot be otherwise. They were not wrong in their view about date and time either, since from the evidence of the Principal, Dupleix College, Chandernagore, it seemed that on the same day and at the same time, Charubabu had taken leave from the College and gone to Calcutta. But the surprising thing was that on that day and at that hour on the Howrah station platform he was found talking with the Mayor of Chandernagore, Tardival, his wife, the Governor of Chandernagore and a few other distinguished European gentlemen. Remembering the occasion they had, all of them, agreed to stand witness in favour of Charubabu. Since the police had to release Charubabu at the instance of the French government, the mystery has remained unsolved. But I would advise Charubabu to send all the proofs to the Psychical Research Society and help in the advancement of knowledge. Police evidence, especially the C.I.D.'s, can never be false, hence there is no way out except to seek refuge in Theosophy. On the whole during this trial at every stage I could find, in the British legal system, how easily the innocent could be punished, sent to prison, suffer transportation, even loss of life. Unless one stands in the dock oneself, one cannot realise the delusive untruth of the Western penal code. It is something of a gamble with human freedom, with man's joys and sorrows, a lifelong agony for him and his family, his friends and relatives, an insult, a living death. In this system there is no counting as to how often guilty persons escape and how many innocent persons perish. Once one has been involved in this game, this cruel, callous, reactionary social machinery, one can understand the reason behind the passionate praise on behalf of Socialism and Anarchism, and their present worldwide influence. In a milieu like this it is not to be wondered at that many liberal and kind-hearted men have started to say: It is better to end and destroy this society; if society has to be preserved with the aid of so much sin and suffering, the burning sighs of the innocent and their hearts' blood, its preservation seems unnecessary.

The only worthwhile event in the magistrate's court was the evidence of Narendranath Goswami. Before describing that event let me first speak about the companions of my days of trouble, the boys who had been accused along with me. Watching their behaviour in the court room I could really feel that a new age had dawned, a new type of children had begun to live on the Mother's lap. Those days the Bengali boys were of two kinds; either docile, well-mannered, harmless, of good character, cowardly, lacking in self-respect and high aims; else they were evil characters, rowdies, restless, cheats, lacking in restraint and honesty. Between these two extremes, creatures of many kinds must have been born in the land of Mother Bengal, but except for eight or ten extraordinarily talented and vigorous pioneers no strong representatives of a superior breed beyond these two groups were usually to be seen. The Bengali had intelligence, talent, but little power of manhood. Looking at these lads, however, one felt as if the liberal, daring, puissant men of an earlier age with a different training had come back to India. That fearless and innocent look in their eyes, the words breathing power, their carefree delighted laughter, even in the midst of great danger the undaunted courage, cheerfulness of mind, absence of despair, or grief, all this was a symptom not of the inert Indians of those days, but of a new age, a new race and a new stir. If these were murderers, then one must say that the bloody shadow of killing had not fallen across their nature, in which there was nothing at all of cruelty, recklessness or bestiality. Without worrying in the least about the future or the outcome of the trial they passed their days in prison with boyish fun, laughter, games, reading and in discussions. Quite early they had made friends with every one, with officers, the sentries, convicts, European sergeants, detectives, court officials and without distinguishing between friends and foes, the high and the low, had started to tell stories and jokes. They found the time spent in the court-room quite tiresome, for in that farce of a trial there was very little that was enjoyable. They had no books with which to beguile the time, and talking was forbidden. Those of them who had started doing yoga, they hadn't so far learnt how to concentrate while in a crowd, for them passing the time proved quite difficult. At first some of them began to bring books with them, this was soon followed by others. Later on one could see a strange spectacle: while the trial was going on, and the fate of thirty or forty accused persons was being wrangled over, whose result might be hanging or transportation for life, some of these accused persons without as much as glancing at what was happening around them, were absorbed in reading the novels of Bankimchandra, Vivekananda's *Raja Yoga* or *Science of Religions*, or the Gita, the Puranas, or European Philosophy. Neither the English sergeants nor the Indian policemen objected to this. They must have thought, if this keeps the caged tigers peaceful, that only lightens our duty. Further, this arrangement harmed no one. But one day Mr. Birley's eyes were drawn to it, to the magistrate this was unbearable. For two or three days he kept quiet, then, he could not hold himself any longer and gave orders forbidding the bringing of books to the court-room. Really, Birley was dispensing justice so beautifully, but instead of everybody enjoying that and listening to his judgements, here was everybody reading books! There was no doubt that this showed great disrespect for Birley's dignity and the majesty of British justice.

During the period of our detention in separate cells, it was only in the police van, an hour or half before the magistrate's arrival and during tiffin time, that we had some scope for conversation. Those who were known to each other from before would employ this recess to avenge the long and forced silence and solitude of the cell and they would spend the time in jokes, pleasantries and a variety of discussions. But the leisure was not conducive to conversation with unfamiliar people, hence I did not talk much. I would listen to their stories and laughter but myself did not join any one other than my brother and Abinash. One person would however often edge his way towards my side, this was the future approver, Narendranath Goswami. He was not quiet and well-behaved, like the other boys, but looked bold, light-hearted and in his character, speech and act was without discipline. At the time of his arrest he had shown his natural courage and forwardness, but being faint-hearted it was impossible for him to put up with the minimum suffering of prison life. A landlord's son, brought up in luxury and evil ways, the severe strain and the austerity of prison life had proved too much, this was a fact which he did not hesitate to express before others. The grotesque longing to be freed by any means from this agony began to grow upon his mind from day to day. At first he had the hope that by withdrawing his confession he might be able to prove that the police had extorted, by torturing him, a confession of his guilt. He told us that his father was determined to procure false witnesses. But within a few days another fact revealed itself. His father and a *moktar*, a pleader's agent, began to visit him frequently in the prison, in the end the detective Shams-ul-Alam also came and started holding long and secret conversions with him. During this period Gossain developed a tendency to be curious and ask all kinds of questions. At this many felt suspicious about him. He would ask big and small questions, of Barindra and Upendra, if they knew or were close to the 'big men of India', and who were the people that helped the secret society with money, and the men belonging to the group outside India and in the different provinces of India, who would run the society now, where were its branches, etc. The news of Gossain's sudden passion for learning soon reached everyone and his intimacy with Shams-ul-Alam too, instead of remaining a confidential love-talk, became an open secret. There was a good deal of comment over this and it was noticed by some that these ever new questions would sprout in Gossain's mind after every visit from the police. It is needless to add that he did not receive satisfactory answers to his questions. When these things were being first talked about among the accused, Gossain himself had confessed that the police were trying to persuade him in a number of ways to turn into a "King's approver". He had once mentioned this to me in the court. "What did you tell them?" "Do you think I am going to listen to that! And even if I do, what do I know that I could offer evidence in the way they would like to have it?" When after a few days he broached the subject once again, I noticed events had moved a bit too far. While standing by my side at the identification parade he told me, "The police are visiting me all the time." "Why don't you tell them that Sir Andrew Frazer was the chief patron of the secret society, that would be ample reward for their labour," I told him jokingly. "I have said something of the sort," answered Gossain. "I have told them that Surendranath Banerjee is our head and that once I had shown him a bomb." Staggered at this I asked, "What was the need of saying that sort of thing?" In answer Gossain said: "I shall make mincemeat of the __ . I have told them many other things of that kind. Let the __ s die of seeking for corroboration. Who knows, because of this the trial may go phut." In answer I only said, "You should give up this kind of mischief. By trying to be clever with them you will be fooled." I do not know how far Gossain had spoken the truth. The other accused thought that he had said all this in order to throw dust in our eyes. To me it seemed that till then Gossain had not wholly made up his mind to turn an approver, even if he had proceeded quite far in that direction, but he had also the hope of spoiling the case by misleading the police. To achieve one's end through trickery and evil ways is the natural inspiration for a wicked disposition. From then on I could make out that, once under the thumb of the police, by telling them fact or fiction, just as they needed, Gossain would try to save his own skin. The degradation of an evil nature were being enacted before our very eyes. I noticed how, from day to day, Gossain's mind was undergoing rapid changes: his face, his movements and manners, his language were not the same as before. He started to adduce economic and political justification in support of ruining his companions through treachery. One does not often come across such an interesting psychological study.

At first no one allowed Gossain to guess that his designs were known to all. He too was so stupid as to be unaware of this for quite some time; he thought he was helping the police quite secretly. But when after a few days it was ordered that instead of solitary confinement we would have to live together, then because of this new arrangement we used to meet and talk throughout the day and night, and the thing could not be a secret much longer. At this time one or two of the boys had quarrels with Gossain. From their language, and the unpleasant behaviour of everybody else, Gossain could see that his intentions were not unknown to any one. When later he gave his evidence before the court, some English newspapers reported that this had caused surprise and excitement among the accused persons. Needless to say, this was entirely the reporters' fancy. Days ahead every one had known the nature of the evidence that would be offered. In fact, even the date on which the evidence would be given was known from before. At this time an accused went to Gossain and said: "Look, brother, life here is intolerable; I too would like to turn an approver. Please tell Shams-ul-Alam to arrange for my release." Gossain agreed to this and after a few days told him that a government note had come to the effect that there might be a possibility of favourable consideration of the accused's appeal. After which Gossain suggested to him to eke out some necessary information from Upen and others, for instance the location of the branches of the secret society and its leaders, etc. The pretended approver was a man with a sense of humour, a lover of fun, and, on Upendra's advice, he supplied a number of imaginary names to Gossain, and said that among the leaders of the secret society were Vishwambhar Pillai in Madras, Purushottam Natekar at Satara, Professor Bhatt in Bombay and Krishnajirao Bhao of Baroda. Gossain was delighted with this and passed on this reliable information to the police. And the police too rummaged the whole of Madras, and came across many Pillais, big and small, but not one that was Pillai Vishwambhar, not even half a Vishwambhar; as for Satara's Purushottam Natekar, he also seemed to keep his identity safely hidden in deep darkness; in Bombay a certain Professor Bhatt was found no doubt, but he seemed a harmless person and a loyalist, there was no likelihood of any secret society using him as a cover. Yet at the time of giving his evidence, Gossain, depending on what he had heard earlier from Upen, offered such ringleaders of conspiracy as the imaginary Vishwambhar Pillai, etc., at the holy feet of Norton and strengthened the latter's strange prosecution theory. With regard to Bir Krishnajirao Bhao the police perpetrated a typical hoax. They produced the copy of a telegram sent by some Ghose from the Manicktola Gardens to Krishnajirao Deshpande of Baroda. The people of Baroda did not know of the existence of any one answering to that name, but since the truthful Gossain had spoken of a Krishnajirao of Baroda, then surely Krishnajirao Bhao and Krishnajirao Deshpande must be the same person. And whether Krishnajirao Deshpande existed or not, the letters mentioned the name of our respected friend, Keshavrao Deshpande. Hence Krishnajirao Bhao and Krishnajirao Deshpande must surely be one and the same. From which it followed that Keshavrao Deshpande was a ringleader of the secret conspiracy. Mr. Norton's famous theory was based on such extraordinary inferences.

To believe Gossain, one had to accept that it was at his suggestion that our solitary confinement had been done away with and we had been ordered to stay together. He had said that the police had arranged it like this and kept him in the midst of the accused with the intention of drawing out secret information about the conspiracy. Gossain did not know that his new business was known to every one long before, when he started to ask questions about those who were engaged in the conspiracy, and the whereabouts of the branches of the secret society, about patrons and contributors, about those who would now be in charge of continuing the secret activities, etc. I have already given examples of the kind of answers he received. But most of Gossain's words were false. Dr. Daly had told us that, by persuading Mr. Emerson, it was he who had brought about this change in our accommodation. Possibly Daly's was the true version; afterwards on hearing about the change in arrangements the police may have imagined this a likely gain. Be it as it may, everyone, excepting me, was extremely pleased at the change. At that period I was unwilling to be in the midst of a crowd, for my spiritual life, *sadhana*, was proceeding at a rapid pace. I had tasted a little of Equality, Non-attachment and Peace, but these states had not been yet fully stabilised. By being in company, with the pressure of other men's thought-waves on my unripe young ideas, this new state of being might suffer, or be even washed away. In fact, it did happen like that. Then I did not understand that for the fullness of my spiritual experience it was necessary to evoke opposite emotions; hence the Inner Guide, *antaryamin*, had suddenly deprived me of my dear solitude, and flung me into the stream of violent outward activity. But the rest of the group went wild with joy. That night, the big room in which singers like Hemchandra Das, Sachindra Sen, etc., were staying, most of the accused persons collected there, and no one had a wink till two or three in the morning. The ring of laughter, the endless stream of singing, all the pent-up stories began to flow like a swollen river during the rainy season. The silent prison reverberated with noise and merriment. In the end we fell asleep but every time we woke up we heard the laughter, the singing, the conversation going on as before. Towards the small hours the stream thinned, the singers too dozed off. Our ward was silent once again.

Prison and Freedom

Men as we are, we are mostly creatures of circumstance, confined to the sensations of the outer world. Our mental activities depend upon such external sensations, even our reason is unable to go beyond the limits of the material; and the joys and sorrows of life are but echoes of outward events. This slavery is due to the domination of the body. In the Upanishad it has been said, "The Self-born has set the doors of the body outwards, therefore the soul of a man gazes outward and not at the self within; hardly a wise man here and there, desiring immortality, turns his gaze inward and sees the Self within him." Normally, the outward, physical eyes with which we observe the life of man, in that kind of seeing the body is our chief support. However much we may call the Europeans materialists, in fact all men are materialists. The body is an instrument for the fulfilment of the religious life, a chariot with many horses to pull it, the body-chariot on which we ride across the ways of the world. But, admitting the false importance of the body we give such a prominence to the physical mind that we find ourselves wholly entangled in outward activity and superficial good and evil. The result of such ignorance is lifelong slavery and subordination. Joys and sorrows, good and evil, affluence and danger, compel us to mould our mental states in their own terms, and we too float along the waves of desire to which we give our thoughts. Greedy of enjoyment and afraid of sorrow, we come to depend on others and, receiving our joys and sorrows from others, we suffer endless misery and humiliation.

Because, be it man or nature, whoever or whatever is able to exercise control over our body, or can bring it within the field of its own forces, we have to submit to that influence. Its extreme example is to fall into the hands of enemies or a life of imprisonment. But the person who, surrounded by friends and boon companions, moves about freely, even his condition is just as wretched as of those who spend their days in prison. The body is the prison, the body-centred intelligence, the reasoning Ignorance is the enemy that imprisons.

This state of imprisonment is the perennial condition of man. On the other hand, on every page of literature and history we find the irrepressible eagerness and enthusiasm on the part of the human race to gain freedom. As in the political and social spheres, so in the life of the individual in every age we find the same endeavour. Restraint, self-torture, indifference, Stoicism, Epicureanism, Asceticism, Vedanta, Buddhism, Advaita, the doctrine of Maya, Raja Yoga, Hatha Yoga, Gita, the Paths of Knowledge, Devotion, and Action – the paths are many, the goal is the same. The aim is always – victory over the body, getting rid of the domination of the physical, the freedom of the inner life. Western scientists have arrived at the conclusion that there is no world other than the physical, the subtle is based on the material, the subtle experiences are but reflections of the external experiences, man's attempt to be free is in vain; the philosophy, religion and Vedanta are but unreal imaginings, and wholly limited by the physical reality and the mind's attempt to untie the knot or cross the limitations of our physical nature is an attempt doomed to fail. But the longing to be free is lodged in such a deep layer of the human heart that a thousand arguments are helpless to uproot it. Man can never remain content with the conclusions of the physical sciences. In all ages he has felt vaguely that the subtle elements capable of conquering the physical limits are definitely to be found in his own inner being, that there is an Inner Controller, a Person for ever free and full of Delight, within him. It is the object of religion to realise this state of eternal freedom and pure Delight. This object of religious seeking is also the object of evolution of which science speaks. Reason or its absence is not the real difference between man and animal. The animal has the power to judge, but in the animal body that power does not develop. The real difference between man and animal lies elsewhere: a complete submission to the body is what constitutes the animal state, while in the conquest of the body and the effort at inner freedom lies man's manhood! This freedom is the chief goal of religion, this is what it calls *mukti*. It is for the sake of *mukti* that through knowledge we try to find out the mental guide of the body and life who lives within, or through action-devotion we try to surrender to it our body, mind and life. The central ethical injunction in the Gita – *yogasthaḥ kuru karmāṇi*[1] – this freedom is that Yoga of the Gita. When the inner joys and sorrows, instead of depending on external good and evil, well-being and danger, become self-generated, self-propelled, self-bound, then the normal human condition is reversed, and the outer life can be modelled on the inner, the bondage of action slackens. The ideal person of the Gita renounces the

[1] Fixed in Yoga do thy actions. *Gita*, II. 48.

desire for the fruit of action and practises active renunciation in the supreme Person, or Purushottama. He is "*duḥkheṣu anudvignamanāḥ sukheṣu vigataspṛhaḥ*",[1] attaining an inner freedom he enjoys self-delight and self-control. Unlike the normal human individual he does not seek, out of fear of sorrow born of longing for pleasure, any external refuge; he does not accept his joys and sorrows from others, and yet is free of the bondage of action. Rather in the battle between Gods and Titans, it is the man, sent by God, greatly controlled, a mightily puissant protagonist, beyond anger and fear, he is the man of yogic action who helps to usher in a political or religious revolution or by preserving the established state and religious order, fulfils in a non-attached spirit God's own work. He is the superior person of whom the Gita speaks.

In the modern times we have arrived at a point of transition between the new and the old. Man is ever moving forward to his goal; from time to time one has to leave the plains and ascend the heights, and it is during these periods of ascent that revolutions occur in the state, society, religion as well as in the spheres of intellect. In the present times there is a preparation, if nothing else, to move towards the subtle from the physical. Because of the minute examination and discovery of the laws of the physical universe by western scientists, the outlying plains surrounding the upward Way have been cleared. The knowers of the West are taking their first step in the vast, inner worlds; many are

[1] He whose mind is undisturbed in the middle of sorrows and amid pleasures is free from desires. *Gita*, II. 30.

tempted by the hope of conquest. Apart from this there are other visible signs – such as the quick spread of Theosophy, the welcome given to Vedanta in America, the partial and indirect influence of India in Western philosophy and modes of thinking. But the most remarkable sign is the sudden and unexpected emergence of India. By claiming the role of world teacher, the Indians are rising to inaugurate a new age. If the Westerners are deprived of the help from India they will not be able to succeed in their efforts at progress. Just as in the cultivation of the supreme means to the flowering of the inner life no country had excelled India in the Knowledge of Brahman or Self (*tattvajñana*) and Yoga, similarly the purification of the nature, the control over the senses, the power of the Brahman-realisation, the energy born of askesis, *tapasya*, and the lesson of non-attached activity as Yoga, these too are India's very own. To acquire, by ignoring the outward joys and sorrows, the inner freedom is possible only for the Indian, the Indian alone is capable of undertaking activity in a spirit of non-attachment, while the sacrifice of ego and indifference in action are acknowledged as the highest aim of her education and culture and are the seed of her national character.

The truth of this view I first realised in the Alipore Jail. Those who live there are usually thieves, robbers, murderers. Though we were forbidden to speak with the convicts, in practice this rule was not strictly observed. Apart from that there were the cook, the waterman, the sweeper, the cleaner, with whom one could not help coming into contact, and many times we would speak freely with each other. Those who were arrested with me for the same offence, they too have been described in such unspeakable terms as the most heartless murderers. If there is any place where the Indian character may be looked upon with eyes of contempt, if it is possible to see it at its worst, lowest and most hateful state, then Alipore Jail is that place, imprisonment at Alipore is that inferior and degenerate state. In such a place I spent twelve months. Thanks to my experience of these twelve months I have been able to return to the world of action with tenfold hope, with a fixed notion about Indian superiority, with redoubled respect for human character, the future progress and well-being of the motherland and the human race. This is not due to my inherent optimism or any excessive trust. Srijut Bipinchandra Pal had felt the same way in the Buxar Jail; in the Alipore Jail, Dr. Daly, who had served there earlier, supported this view. Dr. Daly was a generous and wise person, experienced in the ways of men; the worst elements of human nature were present to him every day, yet he used to tell me: "The more I see and hear of Indian gentlemen or the poor folk, men who are distinguished in society or the convicts in a prison, I am convinced that in quality and character you are much superior to us. Looking at these lads has further confirmed me in my judgement. Who can judge from their behaviour, character and other high qualities that they are anarchists or assassins? Instead of finding in them cruelty, wildness, restlessness or impropriety I find the opposite virtues." Of course thieves and robbers don't turn into holy men while they are serving a term in prison. The British prison is not a place for reform of character; on the contrary, for the ordinary convict it is but an instrument for the degradation of character and manhood. They remain the thieves and robbers that they had been before being sent to gaol; they continue to steal even in the prison, in the midst of the strict prohibitory rules they manage to indulge in addiction, continue to cheat. But what of that? The humanity of the Indian survives every loss. Fallen because of social abuses, crushed out because of loss of humanity, in the outer personality are the distortions of dark, dubious, shameful emotions, yet, within, the nearly vanished humanity seems to save itself in hiding, thanks to the inborn virtue of the Indians, it expresses itself time and again in their speech and act. Those who having seen the filth outside turn away their faces in contempt, only they say that they have failed to find in them the least trace of humanity. But one who has given up the pride of holiness and looks at them with one's own natural clear vision will never agree to such a view. After six months of imprisonment in the Buxar Jail Srijut Bipinchandra Pal had seen God among the thieves and robbers, which he had openly confessed in a meeting at Uttarpara. In the Alipore jail itself I too could realise this fundamental truth of Hinduism for the first time among the thieves, robbers and killers, in the human body I could realise the divine Presence.

In this country who knows how many hundreds of innocent people are undergoing hellish longterm imprisonment and working out the misdeeds of their past lives towards a heavenlier way ahead. But the average westerner, who is not purified by religious emotions and not of a godly nature, how these people fare in such tests, those who live in the western countries or are familiar with their literature expressive of the western mentality and character can easily infer. In a similar situation either their tearful earthly hearts, with their depressive anger and sorrow, move towards hell's murk and, because of the contagion of companions, adopt their cruelty and low ways; else, because of the extreme pressure of weaknesses, lose strength and reasoning power so that what survives is only a remnant of humanity.

Let me speak of an innocent person at Alipore. As an accused in a dacoity case he had been sentenced to ten years' rigorous imprisonment. A cowherd by profession, uneducated, without anything to do with reading or writing, his only support was his faith in God and patience worthy of an Aryan and other noble qualities. Faced with this old man's attitude towards life, my pride of learning and forbearance was completely shattered. There was a serene and simple friendliness written in the old man's eyes, his talk was always full of amiability and friendliness. At times he would speak of his sufferings, even though he was innocent of the charges, and speak of his wife and children. He even wondered when God would bring him release so that he could meet them; but never did I find him depressed or restless. Waiting for God's Grace, he spent his days quietly doing his duties in the prison. His efforts and thoughts were not concerned about himself, but about the well-being of others. His sense of kindness and sympathy for the unfortunate frequently came out in his speech, serving others was the law of his being. The noble qualities were further set off by his humility. Knowing that he had a heart a thousand times nobler than mine, I would feel ashamed at his humility; to accept the old man's service embarassed me, but he would not be deterred so easily. He was all the time anxious about my comfort. As with me, so with the others, his kindly attention and humble service and respect seemed to be much greater especially for the innocent and miserable ones. Yet on his face and in his conduct there glowed a natural serene gravity and majesty. He had a great love for the country, too. I shall always remember the white-whiskered serene visage of this old convict full of kindness and generosity. Even in these days of decline among the Indian peasantry – whom we describe as uneducated, "small people" *(chhotolok)* – may be found such representatives of the Indian race. India's future is hopeful only because of this. The educated youth and the unlettered peasantry, the future of India lies with these two classes. The future Aryan race will be a blend of the two.

I have spoken about an uneducated peasant. Let me now speak of two educated young men. These were the two Kavirajs of Harrison Road, Nagendranath and Dharani.[1] The manner in which, quietly and contentedly they too suffered this sudden mishap, this unjust punishment, was astounding. I could never find in them the slightest anger or censure or annoyance over those for whose fault they had to pass their youth in a hellish prison. They were devoid of the glory of modern education, a knowledge of western languages and familiarity with western learning. The mother-tongue was their only stay, but among the English-educated group I have

[1] Suspecting that the police had come to know of the bombs, Ullaskar, one of the conspirators, had removed a packet containing bombs to his friend Nagendranath's house, who did not know anything about its contents. Later, to save his friend, Ullaskar gave a true confession. But the police did not release the brothers.

– Translator's note

found few men of comparable calibre. Instead of complaining to either man or God, both of them had accepted the punishment with a smile. Both the brothers were *sadhak*s but their natures were different. Nagendra was steady, grave, intelligent. He was very fond of godly conversation and religious topics. When we had been kept in solitary confinement the jail authorities had permitted us, at the end of the day's labour, to read books. Nagendra who had asked for the Gita had been given the Bible instead. In the witness box he would tell me of his feelings on reading the Bible. Nagendra hadn't read the Gita but I noticed with surprise that, instead of speaking about the Bible, he was expressing the inner sense of the Gita's verse – once in a while it even appeared as if the sublime and divine statements of Krishna at Kurukshettra were coming out of the same lotus lips of Vasudeva in the Alipore dock. Without reading the Gita, to be able to realise in the Bible the spirit of equality, renunciation of the desire for fruit, to see the Divine in all things, etc., is the index of a not negligible inner life or spiritual capacity, *sadhana*. Dharani was not as intelligent as Nagendra, but he was obedient and tender by nature, temperamentally a devotee. He was always immersed in the contemplation of divine Motherhood, and looking at the grace that shone on his face, his innocent laughter and gentle devotional attitude, it was hard to realise that we were confined in a jail. Knowing these men, who can say that the Bengali is low and despicable? This power, this manhood, this sacred fire is only hidden amidst the ashes.

They are both innocent. Imprisoned without any fault of their own, by their own qualities or by virtue of their training they had been able to reject the supremacy of external joys and sorrows and succeeded in preserving the freedom of their inner life. But the virtues of the national character came out even among the real offenders. I stayed in Alipore for twelve months, and excepting one or two all the convicts, the thieves, the dacoits and the murderers with whom we had come in contact, we received from all and sundry good behaviour and helpfulness. Rather it was among those spoilt by modern education that these qualities seemed to be lacking. Modern education may have many virtues to recommend itself, but civility and selfless service form no part of these. The kindness and sympathy that are such valuable elements of an Aryan education, I found that even among the thieves and robbers. The sweeper, the cleaner, the waterman – they all had to share, for no fault of their own, part of the misery and hardship of our solitary confinement, but they never expressed to us their anger or annoyance on that score. At times they ventilated their distress before the native jailors, but they would also cheerfully pray for our release from detention. A Mohammedan convict used to love the accused like his own children and at the time of parting he could not restrain himself from shedding tears. Pointing out their suffering and humiliation as the price of patriotism, he would tell others and express his sorrow by saying, "Look, these are gentlemen, sons of the rich, and this their suffering is because they have tried to help the poor and the distressed." Those who vaunt about western culture, I would like to ask them: Is this self-control, charity, generosity, gratitude, godly love for others to be found among the lower order of criminals, the thieves and robbers of England? In fact, Europe is the land of enjoyment; India of sacrifice. The Gita describes two kinds of creatures – *deva* and *asura*. The Indian is intrinsically of the *deva* kind, the westerner of the *asura*. But in this age of deep darkness (*ghor kali*) because of the disappearance of Aryan education, due to the predominance of inertia, in our national decline we are acquiring the inferior qualities of the *asura* while the westerners, because of their national progress and the evolution of manhood, are acquiring the qualities of the *deva*. But in spite of this in their *deva* qualities something of the *asura* and in our *asuric* qualities something of the *deva* can be imperfectly glimpsed. Even the best among them cannot wholly get rid of the *asuric* qualities. When one compares the inferior specimens of both cultures, the truth comes out quite strikingly.

There is much to be written on this topic, but I forbear for fear of the lengthiness of the article. But while I was in the prison those persons in whose bearing I have found this inner freedom, they are the prototypes of the godward emotions, *devabhava*. I have an idea of writing in future an article on this subject.

The Aryan Ideal and the Three Gunas

In the essay entitled "Prison and Freedom" I have, by describing the psychology of some innocent prisoners, tried to establish that, owing to the Aryan discipline, the priceless ancestral legacy of inner freedom which Indians have is not destroyed even in prison – indeed something of the godly disposition, garnered through thousands of years and inherent in the true Aryan character, remains even in the worst of imprisoned criminals. The main principle of the Aryan discipline is the sattwic temperament. He who is sattwic is pure; normally all human beings are impure. This impurity is nourished and increased by the predominance of Rajas and the great density of Tamas. The impurity of mind is of two kinds. First, inertia or impurity due to lack of inclination to work; this is produced by Tamas. Secondly, excitement or impurity due to wrong impulses; this is caused by Rajas. The signs of the mode of Tamas are ignorance, delusion, crudeness of intelligence, unsystematic thinking, laziness, too much sleep, irritation owing to inertia in work, pessimism, despondency, fear – in short, whatever nourishes lack of effort. Inertia and disinclination are the results of ignorance; excitement and bad inclinations, of wrong knowledge. But if the impurity of Tamas is to be removed it can be done only by the increase of Rajas. Rajas is the cause of impulsion and effort and these are the first steps to detachment. He who is inert is not truly detached – the state of inertia is devoid of knowledge; and knowledge indeed is the path of spiritual detachment. He who engages himself in works without desire is detached; mere renunciation of work is not freedom. This is why Swami Vivekananda, noticing the deep tamas of India, used to say, "Rajas is needed, the country needs heroes of action, let the strong current of impulsion flow. Even if evil follows in its wake, it will be a thousand times better than this tamasic inertia."

It is true indeed that sunk in deep Tamas but using Sattwa as an excuse we are pretending and boasting of being highly sattwic. I notice that many people hold the view that we have been conquered by rajasic nations because we are sattwic, that we are degraded and backward because we are spiritual. They try to prove the superiority of Hinduism to Christianity by using that argument. The Christian nations believe in practical results; they try to establish the superiority of a religion by showing the results it produces in this world. They say that the Christian nations are paramount in the world, therefore Christianity is the greatest religion. And many among us argue that this is wrong; it is not possible to decide upon the superiority of a religion by counting what one gains from it in this world; rather its consequences in the next world should be considered; because the Hindus are more religious they are subject to a powerful and titanic nation. But this argument involves a serious mistake which is opposed to the Aryan wisdom. Sattwa can never be the cause of downfall; indeed a nation which is predominantly sattwic cannot remain bound in chains of slavery. The spiritual power of the true Brahmin is the chief result of Sattwa, the prowess of the Kshatriya is the foundation of spiritual power. From calm spiritual power, when it receives a blow, sparks of the prowess of the Kshatriya fly in all directions, everything catches fire as it were. Spiritual power cannot survive where there is no Kshatra-prowess. If there is one true Brahmin in the land he can create a hundred Kshatriyas. The cause of the downfall of this country is not an excess of Sattwa but want of Rajas and preponderance of Tamas. Owing to the lack of Rajas, the Sattwa inherent in us becomes weak and concealed in Tamas. Along with laziness, delusion, ignorance, disinclination, pessimism, despondency and lack of dynamic effort, the sad condition and degradation of the country become worse. This darkness was thin and rare at first; however, in course of time it gradually became so dense, and we, sunk in the obscurity of ignorance, became so utterly devoid of high aspiration and great endeavour, that in spite of the advent of great men sent by God, that darkness has not dispersed entirely. Then the Sun-god decided to save the country through the impulsion roused by Rajas.

It is true that Tamas tends to disappear when Rajas is roused and powerfully active. On the other hand, there is the danger of demoniac qualities like licentiousness, evil impulses, complete lack of restraint, etc. If the force of Rajas operates under its own momentum for the sole satisfaction of large self-assertive inclinations for the fulfilment of wrong ends, then there is enough reason for apprehension. Rajas cannot endure long if it goes along its own path without any control; ennui follows, Tamas appears, as the sky instead of becoming clear is overcast and becomes devoid of the movement of air after a storm. This was the fate of France after the revolution. There was in that revolution a frightful manifestation of Rajas and at the end of it, a resurgence of Tamas to some extent, then another revolution, followed by tiredness, loss of force and more degradation – this is the history of France during the last century. Whenever there arose in the heart of France a sattwic inspiration born of the ideal of liberty, equality and fraternity, Rajas tried to fulfil its own tendencies after gradually becoming predominant and turning itself into a demoniac mode opposed to Sattwa. Consequently, as a result of a reappearance of Tamas, France, having lost its former force, is in a sad and desperate but uncertain state like Harishchandra who stood neither in heaven nor on earth. The only means of avoiding such a result is to engage powerful Rajas in the service of Sattwa. If the sattwic disposition is roused and becomes the guide of Rajas, then there will be no danger of the re-emergence of Tamas, and uncontrolled force, being disciplined and controlled, can do the country and the world a great deal of good according to high ideals. The means to rouse Sattwa is the spiritual temperament – to renounce selfish interests and deploy all one's energies for the good of others – to make the whole of life a great and pure sacrifice by surrendering oneself to the Divine. It is said in the Gita that Sattwa and Rajas together suppress Tamas; Sattwa alone cannot conquer Tamas. This is the reason why God has in modern times spread the force of Rajas all over the land after rousing the religious spirit and the Sattwa inherent in us. Great souls and religious leaders like Rammohan Roy have ushered in a new age by reawakening Sattwa. In the nineteenth century there was not the same awakening in politics and society as in religion. The reason was that the field was not ready. That is why there was no harvest though plenty of seeds were sown. In this also can be seen how kind to and pleased with India God has been. An awakening caused only by Rajas cannot be enduring or completely beneficial. It is necessary to rouse the spiritual force to some extent in the mind and heart of the nation. It is because of this that the current of Rajas was arrested for so long. The manifestation of the force of Rajas since 1905 is full of Sattwic disposition. Owing to this, the tendency towards an uncontrolled enthusiasm does not cause much alarm, since this is the play of Rajas and Sattwa; whatever excitement there is in this will soon be controlled and regulated. Not by any external power but by the inner spiritual force and the sattwic disposition will this be conquered and disciplined. We can only nourish that sattwic temperament by spreading the religious spirit.

I have already said that one of the means of increasing Sattwa is to devote all one's powers to the good of others. And there is plenty of evidence of this spirit in our political awakening. But it is difficult to maintain this spirit. It is difficult for the individual, more so for the nation. Selfish interest, unnoticed, gets mixed up with the good of others and if our understanding is not very pure, we may fall into such a delusion that we may seek only our own selfish ends in the name of service to others and thus sacrifice the good of our fellow-beings, our country and humanity and yet not detect our mistake. Service to God is another means of increasing Sattwa. But even in that path good may turn into its opposite. There may gather in us sattwic apathy towards works after we have achieved the joy of nearness to God. We may turn our back to the service of our distressed land

and humanity. This is the bondage of the sattwic temperament. Just as there is rajasic egoism, so also there is sattwic egoism. Just as sin binds men, so does virtue. There cannot be complete freedom unless we surrender ourselves to God, being fully free from desire and giving up egoism. In order to renounce these two harmful things, we must have pure understanding. To attain mental freedom after eschewing the idea that the body and the spirit are the same is the stage preceding the purification of understanding. When the mind becomes free, then it becomes subject to the soul. After that, conquering the mind and with the help of the understanding, man can to some extent be free from selfishness. Even then it does not cease altogether. The last selfishnes is the desire for spiritual liberation, the wish to be rapt in one's own delight forgetting the misery of others. Even that has to be given up. Its antidote is to realise and serve Narayana in all creatures; this is the perfection of Sattwa. There is still a higher state than this, and that is to take refuge in God utterly by transcending Sattwa and going beyond the modes of Nature. The Gita describes one who is beyond the modes thus:

nānyaṁ guṇebhyaḥ kartāraṁ yadā draṣṭānupaśyati,
guṇebhyaśca paraṃ vetti madbhāvaṁ so'dhigacchati.
guṇānetānatītya trīndehī dehasamudbhavān,
janmamṛtyujarāduḥkhairvimukto 'mṛtamaśnute.
prakāśaṃ ca pravṛttiṁ ca mohameva ca pāṇḍava,
na dveṣṭi sampravṛttāni na nivṛttāni kāṅkṣati.
udāsīnavadāsīno guṇairyo na vicālyate,
guṇa vartanta ityeva yo 'vatiṣṭhati neṅgate.
samaduḥkhasukhaḥ svasthaḥ samaloṣṭāśmakāñcanaḥ,

tulyapriyāpriyo dhīrastulyanindātmasaṁstutiḥ.
mānāpamānayostulyastulyo mitrāripakṣayoḥ,
sarvārambhaparityāgī guṇātītaḥ sa ucyate.
māṁ ca yo 'vyabhicāreṇa bhaktiyogena sevate,
sa guṇān samatītyaitān brahmabhūyāya kalpate.[1]

"When the soul becoming a witness sees the three modes, that is, God's Power of the three modes as the sole doer of all works and also knows the Lord who is beyond the modes and is the mover of Shakti, then he attains the status and nature of the Divine. The embodied soul then transcends the three modes born of the two types of body, namely, the gross and the subtle, and becoming free from birth and death and decay and suffering enjoys immortality. He does not abhor knowledge produced by Sattwa or impulsion caused by Rajas or the clouding of the mind and body created by Tamas, resulting in sloth, torpor and delusion; he remains steadfast like one seated high above maintaining equilibrium in face of the appearance and disappearance of the three modes which cannot disturb him and firm because all these are the modifications born of the intrinsic character of the modes. He to whom happiness and unhappiness, the pleasant and the unpleasant, praise and blame are the same, gold and clod are both like a piece of stone, who is calm and quiet and unshaken within himself, to whom honour and insult are alike and friend and enemies are equally dear, who does not do anything by his own initiative, but does all works surrendering them to the Divine and only under His

[1] The Gita, chap. XIV, verses 19, 20, 22-26.

inspiration, is described as one above the modes. He who worships Me by the yoga of faultless love and devotion becomes fit to attain the Brahman by going beyond the three modes."

Though this state beyond the Gunas is not attainable by all, it is not impossible for the pre-eminently sattwic man to achieve the state preceding it. The first step to that is to give up sattwic egoism and to see in all action the play of the Divine's Power of the three Gunas. Knowing this, the sattwic worker renounces the idea that he is the doer and does all his works surrendering himself to God.

What we have said about the Gunas and transcendence of them is the fundamental teaching of the Gita. But this teaching has not been widely accepted. Till now what we have known as the Aryan education has been mostly the cultivation of the sattwic temperament. The appreciation of the rajasic mode has come to an end in this country with the disintegration of the Kshatriya order. And yet there is a great need for the Rajas-force in national life. That is why the attention of the nation has again been drawn to the Gita. The teaching of the Gita, though based on the ancient Aryan wisdom, goes beyond it. Its practical teaching is not afraid of the Rajas quality, there is in it the way to press Rajas into the service of Sattwa and also the means of spiritual liberation even through the path of works. How the mind of the nation is being prepared for the practice of this teaching I could first understand while in jail. The current is still not clean but contaminated and impure; but when its excessive force slows down a little, then there will be the action of the pure Energy in it.

Many of those who were accused of the same offence as myself and were in jail with me have been acquitted as not guilty. Others have been convicted of being involved in a conspiracy. There is in human society no graver crime than killing. The personal character of the man who commits murder in the interest of the nation may not be blackened. But that does not lessen the gravity of the crime from the social point of view. It must also be admitted that there is an impression of killing upon the inner being, there is as it were a blood-stain on the mind, an invasion by cruelty. Cruelty is a characteristic of the savage, the foremost among those from which mankind is becoming free in evolutionary upward progress. A dangerous thorn will be uprooted from the path of the ascent of humanity if we can renounce it completely. If we assume the guilt of those who have been accused, it must be understood that it is only an excessive but temporary and uncontrolled manifestation of Rajas-force. There is in them such hidden sattwic force that this temporary lack of discipline is not a cause for alarm.

The inner freedom I have mentioned before was a natural quality of my companions. During the days we were lodged together in a big verandah, I observed with great attention their conduct and psychological dispositions. Apart from two of them, I never saw even a trace of fear in the face or speech of anyone. Almost all were young men, many mere boys. Even strong-minded people were likely to be very upset at the thought of the dire punishment to be given to the accused if found guilty. And these young men did not really hope to be acquitted at the trial. Especially, on observing the frightful paraphernalia of witnesses and written evidence at the court, people not versed in law would have easily got the idea that even the innocent could not find a way of escape from that net. Yet instead of fear or despondency on their faces there were only cheerfulness, the smile of simplicity and, forgetting their own danger, discussion about their country and religion. A small library grew up as everyone in our ward had a few books with him. Most books in the library were religious – the Gita, the Upanishads, the works of Vivekananda, the life and conversations of Ramakrishna, the Puranas, hymns, spiritual songs, etc. Among other volumes were the works of Bankim, patriotic songs, books on European philosophy, history and literature. A few of the men practised spiritual disciplines in the morning, some used to read books, still others to chat quietly. Occasionally there were roars of laughter in the peaceful atmosphere of the morning. If the court was not in session, some slept, a few played games – it might be anything, nobody was attached to a particular one. On some days, a quiet game with people sitting in a circle, on others, running and jumping; there was football for a few days, though the ball was made of a unique material; blind-man's-buff was played on some days, on others a number of groups were formed for lessons in ju-jitsu, high and long jumping or for playing draughts. Except a few reserved and elderly people everybody joined in these games at the request of the boys. I observed that even those who were not young had a childlike character. In the evenings there were musical soirées. Only patriotic and religious songs were sung; we used to sit around and hear Ullas, Sachindra, Hemdas, who were accomplished singers; on some evenings, for amusement, Ullaskar sang comic songs or acted, ventriloquised, mimed, or told stories about hemp addicts .... Nobody paid any attention to the trial, all passed the days in religious pursuits or in just being gay. This unperturbed disposition is impossible for one used to evil actions; there was not the slightest trace in them of harshness, cruelty, habitual evil-doing or crookedness. Laughter, conversation or play, all was joyful, sinless, full of love.

The result of this freedom of the mind began to show itself soon. The perfect fruit can be obtained only if the spiritual seed is sown in this kind of field. Pointing at some boys Jesus said to the disciples, "Those who are like these boys will attain the Kingdom of God." Knowledge and delight are the signs of Sattwa. They alone have the capacity for Yoga who do not consider misery as misery but are full of joy and cheer in all situations. The rajasic attitude does not get any encouragement in jail and there is nothing there to nourish the tendency to worldly pleasures. Under these circumstances, since there is a dearth of things to which it is used and in which its Rajas can be indulged, the demoniac mind destroys itself like a tiger. There follows what the Western poets call "eating one's own heart." The Indian mind when in seclusion, though there be external suffering, turns through an eternal attraction to God. This is what happened with us too. A current, I do not know from where, just swept us all. Even people who had never taken God's name learnt to practise some spiritual discipline and realising the grace of the most Gracious became steeped in joy. Those boys achieved in a few months what Yogis take a long time to attain. Ramakrishna Paramahamsa once said, "What you are seeing now is really nothing – such a flood of spirituality is coming into this land that even boys will attain realisation after three days' Sadhana." To see these boys was to have no doubt about the truth of this prophecy. They were as it were the manifest precursors of that spiritual flood. The sattwic waves overflowing the prisoners' docks swept over all, except four or five persons, with great joy. Anyone who has tasted that once cannot forget it nor can he acknowledge any other joy as comparable. This sattwic temperament is indeed the hope of the country. The ease with which brotherliness, self-knowledge and love of God possess the Indian mind and express themselves in action is not possible in the case of any other nation. What is necessary is the renunciation of Tamas, the control of Rajas and the manifestation of Sattwa. This is what is being prepared for India in accordance with God's secret purpose.

New Birth

In the Gita Arjuna asks Sri Krishna: "He who takes up yoga but before going through to the end, wanders away and falls from it, what happens to him? Does he lose both worldly and spiritual gains and perish like a cloud dissolving?" In answer Sri Krishna says: "Neither in this life nor hereafter is there destruction for him. Never does any one who practises good come to woe. Having attained to the world of the righteous and having dwelt there for immemorial years, he who fell from yoga is again born in the house of such as are pure and glorious and, driven by his longing for yoga acquired during past lives, he tries even more for perfection and, finally, through the practice of many lives gets rid of all sins and achieves the supreme end."

The theory of re-incarnation, which has been always held in the Aryan religion as a part of the knowledge acquired through yoga, had lost its position among the educated fold due to the influence of western learning. After the advent (*lila*) of Sri Ramakrishna and the spread of Vedantic knowledge and the study of the Gita that truth is being re-established. Just as heredity is the chief truth of the physical world, so, in the subtle world, re-incarnation is the chief truth. There are two truths implied in Sri Krishna's statement. Persons who have fallen from the path of yoga are born with the tendencies (*samskaras*) of learning acquired in their past lives, and, like a boat moved by the wind, are brought by these tendencies to the path of yoga. But, in order to achieve results, for the taking up of a suitable body it is necessary to be born into a family that is fit and proper. An excellent heredity produces a fit body. When one is born in a pure and glorious home, one has a pure and strong body; born in a family of yogis one has an excellent body and mind and has the advantage of the requisite education and mentality.

For the past few years in India one can see as if a new race being created in the midst of the old that was dominated by the gross influences. The earlier children of Mother India were born in an irreligious atmosphere or one of religious decline and, receiving an education in keeping with that, they had grown short-lived, small, selfish and narrow in spirit. Many powerful great souls were born among these people and it is they who have saved the race in its hour of great peril. But without doing work commensurate with their energy and genius, they have only created a field for the future greatness and the marvellous activity that awaits this race. It is because of their good deeds that the rays of the new dawn are brightening up all the corners. These new children of Mother India, instead of getting the qualities of their parents, have grown bold, full of power, high-souled, self-sacrificing, inspired by the high ideals of helping others and doing good to the country. That is why, instead of being obedient to their parents, the young men go their own way, there is a difference between the old and the young, and in deciding a course of activity there is a conflict between the two. The old are trying to keep these youth, born of divine emanations, the pioneers of a golden age, confined to the old, selfish and narrow ways, without understanding they are trying to perpetuate the Age of Iron. The youth are sparks born of the Great

Energy, *Mahashakti*, eager to build the new by destroying the old, they are unable to be obedient or submit to the laws of respect for the parent. God alone can remedy this discordance. But the will of the Great Energy cannot be in vain, the new generation will not leave without fulfilling the purpose for which they have come. In the midst of the new the influence of the old lingers on. Because of the fault of inferior heredity and an *asuric* education many black sheep have also taken birth; and those who have been ordained to inaugurate the new age are unable to manifest their inherent force and strength. Among the youth is a marvellous sign of manifesting the Age of Gold, a religious bent of mind, and in the hearts of many, a longing for yoga and half-expressed yogic powers.

Ashok Nandi, accused in the Alipore Bomb Conspiracy Case, belongs to this second category. Those who know him would hardly believe that he could be involved in any conspiracy. He had been sentenced on slender and rather incredible evidence. He was not overwhelmed, like the other young people, by a strong desire to serve the national cause. In intellect, character and life he was wholly a yogi and devotee, he had none of the qualities of a man of the world. His grandfather was a realised Tantric yogi (*siddha*), his father too was known to have acquired powers through the pursuit of yoga. The rare birth in a family of yogis of which the Gita speaks, that had been his good fortune. Signs of his inherent yogic powers had shown themselves intermittently even at a tender age. Long before his arrest he had come to know that he was destined to die while young, hence his mind did not take seriously to schooling or the preliminaries of leading a worldly life; yet on his father's advice, ignoring the decree of fate of which he knew already, he pursued what he considered to be his duty and had taken to the path of yoga. It was then that he was suddenly arrested. Ashok remained unperturbed at this danger brought upon him by his destiny and in the jail he devoted all his energies to the pursuit of yoga. Many of the accused in the case had adopted this path, and though not foremost he was one among these. In love and devotion he was inferior to none. His generous character, sober devotion and loving heart charmed everyone. At the time of Gossain's murder he had already been ailing in hospital. Placed in solitary confinement before he could fully recover, he suffered frequently from fever. Even when sick he had to stay during the chilly nights in a room that was open on all sides. Because of this he developed tuberculosis and then, when there was no chance of his surviving, sentenced to the heaviest punishment, he was kept once again in that death-cell. Thanks to the petition of the barrister Chittaranjan Das arrangements were made to remove him to the hospital, but he was not given bail. In the end, due to the Governor's generosity, he was allowed to die in his own home, looked after by his own people. Before he could be freed through appeal God released him from the body's prison. Towards the end Ashok's yogic powers developed considerably; on the day of his passing away, absorbed in the power of Lord Vishnu, he spoke of the holy, salvation-inducing Name and gave spiritual advice to others before giving up the body with the Name on his lips. Ashok Nandi had been born to work out the consequences due to a previous incarnation, hence all this misery and his untimely death. The energy needed to usher in the Age of Gold did not descend in him, but he has shown a brilliant example of the natural yogic powers. Men of good deeds spend a little time in this world to work out their previous sins, then, freed from all sins, they leave the defective body and, assuming another body, they come to express their inherent energies and to do good to men and creatures.

Invitation

With wind and the weather beating round me
  Up to the hill and the moorland I go.
Who will come with me? Who will climb with me?
  Wade through the brook and tramp through the snow?

Not in the petty circle of cities
  Cramped by your doors and your walls I dwell;
Over me God is blue in the welkin,
  Against me the wind and the storm rebel.

I sport with solitude here in my regions,
  Of misadventure have made me a friend.
Who would live largely? Who would live freely?
  Here to the wind-swept uplands ascend.

I am the lord of tempest and mountain,
  I am the Spirit of freedom and pride.
Stark must he be and a kinsman to danger
  Who shares my kingdom and walks at my side.

(*Composed in Alipore Jail, 1908-09*)

Uttarpara Speech

When I was asked to speak to you at the annual meeting of your Sabha, it was my intention to say a few words about the subject chosen for today, the subject of the Hindu religion. I do not know now whether I shall fulfil that intention; for as I sat here, there came into my mind a word that I have to speak to you, a word that I have to speak to the whole of the Indian Nation. It was spoken first to myself in jail and I have come out of jail to speak it to my people.

It was more than a year ago that I came here last. When I came I was not alone; one of the mightiest prophets of Nationalism sat by my side. It was he who then came out of the seclusion to which God had sent him, so that in the silence and solitude of his cell he might hear the word that He had to say. It was he that you came in your hundreds to welcome. Now he is far away, separated from us by thousands of miles. Others whom I was accustomed to find working beside me are absent. The storm that swept over the country has scattered them far and wide. It is I this time who have spent one year in seclusion, and now that I come out I find all changed. One who always sat by my side and was associated in my work is a prisoner in Burma; another is in the north rotting in detention. I looked round when I came out, I looked round for those to whom I had been accustomed to look for counsel and inspiration. I did not find them. There was more than that. When I went to jail the whole country was alive with the cry of Bande Mataram, alive with the hope of a nation, the hope of millions of men who had newly risen out of degradation. When I came out of jail I listened for that cry, but there was instead a silence. A hush had fallen on the country and men seemed bewildered; for instead of God's bright heaven full of the vision of the future that had been before us, there seemed to be overhead a leaden sky from which human thunders and lightnings rained. No man seemed to know which way to move, and from all sides came the question, "What shall we do next? What is there that we can do?" I too did not know which way to move, I too did not know what was next to be done. But one thing I knew, that as it was the Almighty Power of God which had raised that cry, that hope, so it was the same Power which had sent down that silence. He who was in the shouting and the movement was also in the pause and the hush. He has sent it upon us, so that the nation might draw back for a moment and look into itself and know His will. I have not been disheartened by that silence, because I had been made familiar with silence in my prison and because I knew it was in the pause and the hush that I had myself learned this lesson through the long year of my detention. When Bepin Chandra Pal came out of jail, he came with a message, and it was an inspired message. I remember the speech he made here. It was a speech not so much political as religious in its bearing and intention. He spoke of his realisation in jail, of God within us all, of the Lord within the nation, and in his subsequent speeches also he spoke of a greater than ordinary force in the movement and a greater than ordinary purpose before it. Now I also meet you again, I also come out of jail, and again it is you of Uttarpara who are the first to welcome me, not at a political meeting but at a meeting of a society for the protection of our religion. That message which Bepin Chandra Pal received in Buxar jail, God gave to me in Alipore. That knowledge He gave to me day after day during my twelve months of imprisonment and it is that which He has commanded me to speak to you now that I have come out.

I knew I would come out. The year of detention was meant only for a year of seclusion and of training. How could anyone hold me in jail longer than was necessary for God's purpose? He had given me a word to speak and a work to do, and until that word was spoken I knew that no human power could hush me, until that work was done no human power could stop God's instrument, however weak that instrument might be or however small. Now that I have come out, even in these few minutes, a word has been suggested to me which I had no wish to speak. The thing I had in my mind He has thrown from it and what I speak is under an impulse and a compulsion.

When I was arrested and hurried to the Lal Bazar *hājat* I was shaken in faith for a while, for I could not look into the heart of His intention. Therefore I faltered for a moment and cried out in my heart to Him, "What is this that has happened to me? I believed that I had a mission to work for the people of my country and until that work was done, I should have Thy protection. Why then am I here and on such a charge?" A day passed and a second day and a third, when a voice came to me from within, "Wait and see." Then I grew calm and waited, I was taken from Lal Bazar to Alipore and was placed for one month in a solitary cell apart from men. There I waited day and night for the voice of God within me, to know what He had to say to me, to learn what I had to do. In this seclusion the earliest realisation, the first lesson came to me. I remembered then that a month or more before my arrest, a call had come to me to put aside all activity, to go into seclusion and to look into myself, so that I might enter into closer communion with Him. I was weak and could not accept the call. My work was very dear to me and in the pride of my heart I thought that unless I was there, it would suffer or even fail and cease; therefore I would not leave it. It seemed to me that He spoke to me again and said, "The bonds you had not the strength to break, I have broken for you, because it is not my will nor was it ever my intention that that should continue. I have had another thing for you to do and it is for that I have brought you here, to teach you what you could not learn for yourself and to train you for my work." Then He placed the Gita in my hands. His strength entered into me and I was able to do the sadhana of the Gita. I was not only to understand intellectually but to realise what Sri Krishna demanded of Arjuna and what He demands of those who aspire to do His work, to be free from repulsion and desire, to do work for Him without the demand for fruit, to renounce self-will and become a passive and faithful instrument in His hands, to have an equal heart for high and low, friend and opponent, success and failure, yet not to do His work negligently. I realised what the Hindu religion meant. We speak often of the Hindu religion, of the Sanatan Dharma, but few of us really know what that religion is. Other religions are preponderatingly religions of faith and profession, but the Sanatan Dharma is life itself; it is a thing that has not so much to be believed as lived. This is the Dharma that for the salvation of humanity was cherished in the seclusion of this peninsula from of old. It is to give this religion that India is rising. She does not rise as other countries do, for self or when she is strong, to trample on the weak. She is rising to shed the eternal light entrusted to her over the world. India has always existed for humanity and not for herself and it is for humanity and not for herself that she must be great.

Therefore this was the next thing He pointed out to me, – He made me realise the central truth of the Hindu religion. He turned the hearts of my jailors to me and they spoke to the Englishman in charge of the jail, "He is suffering in his confinement; let him at least walk outside his cell for half an hour in the morning and in the evening." So it was arranged, and it was while I was walking that His strength again entered into me. I looked at the jail that secluded me from men and it was no longer by its high walls that I was imprisoned; no, it was Vasudeva who surrounded me. I walked under the branches of the tree in front of my cell but it was not the tree, I knew it was Vasudeva, it was Sri Krishna whom I saw standing there and holding over me his shade. I looked at the bars of my cell, the very grating that did duty for a door and again I saw Vasudeva. It was Narayana who was guarding and standing sentry over me. Or I lay on the coarse blankets that were given me for a couch and felt the arms of Sri Krishna around me, the arms of my Friend and Lover. This was the first use of the deeper vision He gave me. I looked at the prisoners in the jail, the thieves, the murderers, the swindlers, and as I looked at them I saw Vasudeva, it was Narayana whom I found in these darkened souls and misused bodies. Amongst these thieves and dacoits there were many who put me to shame by their sympathy, their kindness, the humanity triumphant over such adverse circumstances. One I saw among them especially, who seemed to me a saint, a peasant of my nation who did not know how to read and write, an alleged dacoit sentenced to ten years' rigorous imprisonment, one of those whom we look down upon in our Pharisaical pride of class as Chhotalok. Once more He spoke to me and said, "Behold the people among whom I have sent you to do a little of my work. This is the nature of the nation I am raising up and the reason why I raise them."

When the case opened in the lower court and we were brought before the Magistrate I was followed by the same insight. He said to me, "When you were cast into jail, did not your heart fail and did you not cry out to me, where is Thy protection? Look now at the Magistrate, look now at the Prosecuting Counsel." I looked and it was not the Magistrate whom I saw, it was Vasudeva, it was Narayana who was sitting there on the bench. I looked at the Prosecuting Counsel and it was not the Counsel for the prosecution that I saw; it was Sri Krishna who sat there, it was my Lover and Friend who sat there and smiled. "Now do you fear?" He said, "I am in all men and I overrule their actions and their words. My protection is still with you and you shall not fear. This case which is brought against you, leave it in my hand. It is not for you. It was not for the trial that I brought you here but for something else. The case itself is only a means for my work and nothing more." Afterwards when the trial opened in the Sessions Court, I began to write many instructions for my Counsel as to what was false in the evidence against me and on what points the witnesses might be cross-examined. Then something happened which I had not expected. The arrangements which had been made for my defence were suddenly changed and another Counsel stood there to defend me. He came unexpectedly, – a friend of mine, but I did not know he was coming. You have all heard the name of the man who put away from him all other thoughts and abandoned all his practice, who sat up half the night day after day for months and broke his health to save me, – Srijut Chittaranjan Das. When I saw him, I was satisfied, but I still thought it necessary to write instructions. Then all that was put away from me and I had the message from within, "This is the man who will save you from the snares put around your feet. Put aside those papers. It is not you who will instruct him. I will instruct him." From that time I did not of myself speak a word to my Counsel about the case or give a single instruction, and if ever I was asked a question, I always found that my answer did not help the case. I had left it to him and he took it entirely into his hands, with what result you know. I knew all along what He meant for me, for I heard it again and again, always I listened to the voice within; "I am guiding, therefore fear not. Turn to your own work for which I have brought you to jail and when you come out, remember never to fear, never to hesitate. Remember that it is I who am doing this, not you nor any other. Therefore whatever clouds may come, whatever dangers and sufferings, whatever difficulties, whatever impossibilities, there is nothing impossible, nothing difficult. I am in the nation and its uprising and I am Vasudeva, I am Narayana, and what I will, shall be, not what others will. What I choose to bring about, no human power can stay."

Meanwhile He had brought me out of solitude and placed me among those who had been accused along with me. You have spoken much today of my self-sacrifice and devotion to my country. I have heard that kind of speech ever since I came out of jail, but I hear it with embarrassment, with something of pain. For I know my weakness, I am a prey to my own faults and back-slidings. I was not blind to them before and when they all rose up against me in seclusion, I felt them utterly. I knew then that I the man was a mass of weakness, a faulty and imperfect instrument, strong only when a higher strength entered into me. Then I found myself among these young men and in many of them I discovered a mighty courage, a power of self-effacement in comparison with which I was simply nothing. I saw one or two who were not only superior to me in force and character, – very many were that, – but in the promise of that intellectual ability on which I prided myself. He said to me, "This is the young generation, the new and mighty nation that is arising at my command. They are greater than yourself. What have you to fear? If you stood aside or slept, the work would still be done. If you were cast aside tomorrow, here are the young men who will take up your work and do it more mightily than you have ever done. You have only got some strength from me to speak a word to this nation which will help to raise it." This was the next thing He told me.

Then a thing happened suddenly and in a moment I was hurried away to the seclusion of a solitary cell. What

Defence Counsel Chittaranjan Das

happened to me during that period I am not impelled to say, but only this that day after day, He showed me His wonders and made me realise the utter truth of the Hindu religion. I had had many doubts before. I was brought up in England amongst foreign ideas and an atmosphere entirely foreign. About many things in Hinduism I had once been inclined to believe that they were imaginations, that there was much of dream in it, much that was delusion and Maya. But now day after day I realised in the mind, I realised in the heart, I realised in the body the truths of the Hindu religion. They became living experiences to me, and things were opened to me which no material science could explain. When I first approached Him, it was not entirely in the spirit of the Bhakta, it was not entirely in the spirit of the Jnani. I came to Him long ago in Baroda some years before the Swadeshi began and I was drawn into the public field.

When I approached God at that time, I hardly had a living faith in Him. The agnostic was in me, the atheist was in me, the sceptic was in me and I was not absolutely sure that there was a God at all. I did not feel His presence. Yet something drew me to the truth of the Vedas, the truth of the Gita, the truth of the Hindu religion. I felt there must be a mighty truth somewhere in this Yoga, a mighty truth in this religion based on the Vedanta. So when I turned to the Yoga and resolved to practise it and find out if my idea was right, I did it in this spirit and with this prayer to Him, "If Thou art, then thou knowest my heart. Thou knowest that I do not ask for Mukti, I do not ask for anything which others ask for. I ask only for strength to uplift this nation, I ask only to be allowed to live and work for this people whom I love and to whom I pray that I may devote my life." I strove long for the realisation of Yoga and at last to some extent I had it, but in what I most desired I was not satisfied. Then in the seclusion of the jail, of the solitary cell I asked for it again. I said, "Give me Thy Adesh. I do not know what work to do or how to do it. Give me a message." In the communion of Yoga two messages came. The first message said, "I have given you a work and it is to help to uplift this nation. Before long the time will come when you will have to go out of jail; for it is not my will that this time either you should be convicted or that you should pass the time, as others have to do, in suffering for their country. I have called you to work, and that is the Adesh for which you have asked. I give you the Adesh to go forth and do my work." The second message came and it said, "Something has been shown to you in this year of seclusion, something about which you had your doubts and it is the truth of the Hindu religion. It is this religion that I am raising up before the world, it is this that I have perfected and developed through the Rishis, saints and Avatars, and now it is going forth to do my work among the nations. I am raising up this nation to send forth my word. This is the Sanatan Dharma, this is the eternal religion which you did not really know before, but which I have now revealed to you. The agnostic and the sceptic in you have been answered, for I have given you proofs within and without you, physical and subjective, which have satisfied you. When you go forth, speak to your nation always this word, that it is for the Sanatan Dharma that they arise, it is for the world and not for themselves that they arise. I am giving them freedom for the service of the world. When therefore it is said that

India shall rise, it is the Sanatan Dharma that shall rise. When it is said that India shall be great, it is the Sanatan Dharma that shall be great. When it is said that India shall expand and extend herself, it is the Sanatan Dharma that shall expand and extend itself over the world. It is for the Dharma and by the Dharma that India exists. To magnify the religion means to magnify the country. I have shown you that I am everywhere and in all men and in all things, that I am in this movement and I am not only working in those who are striving for the country but I am working also in those who oppose them and stand in their path. I am working in everybody and whatever men may think or do, they can do nothing but help in my purpose. They also are doing my work, they are not my enemies but my instruments. In all your actions you are moving forward without knowing which way you move. You mean to do one thing and you do another. You aim at a result and your efforts subserve one that is different or contrary. It is Shakti that has gone forth and entered into the people. Since long ago I have been preparing this uprising and now the time has come and it is I who will lead it to its fulfilment."

This then is what I have to say to you. The name of your society is "Society for the Protection of Religion". Well, the protection of the religion, the protection and upraising before the world of the Hindu religion, that is the work before us. But what is the Hindu religion? What is this religion which we call Sanatan, eternal? It is the Hindu religion only because the Hindu nation has kept it, because in this Peninsula it grew up in the seclusion of the sea and the Himalayas, because in this sacred and ancient land it was given as a charge to the Aryan race to preserve through the ages. But it is not circumscribed by the confines of a single country, it does not belong peculiarly and for ever to a bounded part of the world. That which we call the Hindu religion is really the eternal religion, because it is the universal religion which embraces all others. If a religion is not universal, it cannot be eternal. A narrow religion, a sectarian religion, an exclusive religion can live only for a limited time and a limited purpose. This is the one religion that can triumph over materialism by including and anticipating the discoveries of science and the speculations of philosophy. It is the one religion which impresses on mankind the closeness of God to us and embraces in its compass all the possible means by which man can approach God. It is the one religion which insists every moment on the truth which all religions acknowledge that He is in all men and all things and that in Him we move and have our being. It is the one religion which enables us not only to understand and believe this truth but to realise it with every part of our being. It is the one religion which shows the world what the world is, that it is the Lila of Vasudeva. It is the one religion which shows us how we can best play our part in that Lila, its subtlest laws and its noblest rules. It is the one religion which does not separate life in any smallest detail from religion, which knows what immortality is and has utterly removed from us the reality of death.

This is the word that has been put into my mouth to speak to you today. What I intended to speak has been put away from me, and beyond what is given to me I have nothing to say. It is only the word that is put into me that I can speak to you. That word is now finished. I spoke once before with this force in me and I said then that this movement is not a political movement and that nationalism is not politics but a religion, a creed, a faith. I say it again today, but I put it in another way. I say no longer that nationalism is a creed, a religion, a faith; I say that it is the Sanatan Dharma which for us is nationalism. This Hindu nation was born with the Sanatan Dharma, with it it moves and with it it grows. When the Sanatan Dharma declines, then the nation declines, and if the Sanatan Dharma were capable of perishing, with the Sanatan Dharma it would perish. The Sanatan Dharma, that is nationalism. This is the message that I have to speak to you.

NOTE ON THE TEXTS

Tales of Prison Life. Bengali original. First published under the title *Karakahini* in the Calcutta monthly journal *Suprabhat* in 1316 B.S. (1909-10). First edition 1328 B.S. (1921-22). Second edition 1967. Third edition 1982 as part of the volume *Sri Aurobinder Bangla Rachana*. Translation of Sisir Kumar Ghosh of Shantiniketan, West Bengal, first published in the 1968 issue of *Sri Aurobindo Mandir Annual* (journal of Sri Aurobindo Pathmandir, Calcutta). First edition 1974. Second edition 1979. Third edition 1985. Fourth edition 1997, enlarged by the inclusion of the material listed below.

Prison and Freedom. Bengali original. First published in the journal *Bharati*, c. 1909. Translator unknown. Translation first published in *Sri Aurobindo Mandir Annual*, 1968.

The Aryan Ideal and the Three Gunas. Bengali original. First published in the journal *Dharma*, c. 1909. Translation by Arabinda Basu of Sri Aurobindo Ashram, Pondicherry, first published in *Sri Aurobindo Mandir Annual*, 1968.

New Birth. Bengali original. First published in the journal *Dharma*, c. 1909. Translator unknown. Translation first published in *Sri Aurobindo Mandir Annual*, 1968.

Invitation. English original. Composed in Alipore Jail and later written down from memory. First published in *Karmayogin*, a Calcutta weekly edited and largely written by Sri Aurobindo, 6 November 1909.

Uttarapara Speech. English original. First published in the Calcutta daily *The Bengalee*, 1 June 1909; republished, thoroughly revised by Sri Aurobindo, in *Karmayogin*, 19 June 1909. First edition 1919.